A HISTORY
OF GARDENING
IN SCOTLAND

FIG. I.—A SCOTTISH GARDEN TO-DAY. A PORTION OF THE HERBACEOUS
BORDER AT BALLUMBIE IN ANGUS

A HISTORY
OF GARDENING
IN SCOTLAND

by

E. H. M. COX

Illustrated

LONDON
CHATTO & WINDUS
1935
for New Flora & Silva Ltd.

PRINTED IN GREAT BRITAIN BY
R. & R. CLARK, LIMITED
EDINBURGH

PREFACE

In a book of this kind, where information is often difficult to come by, the author is forced, willy-nilly, to become a nuisance to his friends and a bother to complete strangers. To friend and stranger I can but apologize and hope that the result is worth the trouble I have caused them.

Unfortunately in this case the number is so large that I cannot mention them all by name.

I have to thank the Duke of Buccleuch for his kind permission to examine the estate accounts of Dalkeith and to reproduce the old plan of the Dalkeith garden; and also to Mr James Ormiston of Dalkeith for his assistance in my researches in the Dalkeith papers. I am much indebted to the Earl of Home for information about The Hirsel and for permission to reproduce the photograph of old ribbon bedding in that garden, and also to Lord Hamilton of Dalzell for much interesting data about Dalzell. The Honourable Mrs Stirling has been unfailing in her help over the fine Victorian gardens at Keir.

Then I am much beholden to the Director of the National Gallery of Scotland, to Dr. Meikle, Librarian of the National Library, the Librarian of the Royal Botanic Garden, Edinburgh, the Librarian of the Paisley Free Library, and particularly to Dom Placid Corballis, Librarian of the Benedictine Monastery of Fort Augustus, who has been of the greatest assistance in the section on Monastic Gardens.

Many nurserymen have given freely of their information, and I am grateful to them; among them Mr Archibald Forbes, Mr W. P. Laird, Mr A. R. Lemon, and particularly to Mr J. H. Alexander of Messrs Dicksons & Company for allowing me to examine the daybook of his forebear, and to Mr John Cairns of Messrs Austin & McAslan, Ltd., for lending me the interesting correspondence between Austin and Aiton. I also thank the Editor of *Country Life* for his kind permission to reproduce the photographs of the gardens at Barncluith, Drumlanrig, Drummond Castle and Stobhall.

Nearer at home I offer sincere thanks to Mr A. S. Webster, Chief Librarian, and Mr J. D. Dundas, Sub-Librarian of the Dundee Free Library, for their unfailing courtesy and help; and finally to Mr Frank Buist for his many excellent suggestions.

E. H. M. COX

BROUGHTY FERRY
September 1935

CONTENTS

ILLUSTRATIONS

xi

INTRODUCTION

In recording the story of gardening in Scotland the historian can look with envy on the history of gardening south of the Border. In England from first to last there is ample material. There is an abundant literature on the subject, old gardening books, family papers, travellers' descriptions, diaries; indeed, one of the difficulties in writing a history of English gardening must be to sift the grain from the chaff. Above all, there were gardens in plenty.

In Scotland, on the other hand, there is lack of the written word; there was no gardening book before 1683; family papers rarely deal with the subject; accounts of early travellers are mainly concerned with the lack of the simplest amenities of civilization. The truth is that gardening, as we know it, was little practised in Scotland before the accession of James VI.

The history of early domestic life in Scotland suffers from lack of records. The Register House and Parliament House in Edinburgh contain masses of documents, but they consist mostly of official papers and accounts, written with a soul-destroying preciseness and lacking the personal element which is so invaluable in reconstructing the everyday life of a people. It is doubly unfortunate that the muniments of the great families, where they exist, consist of the same class of legal document. The important fact is that with the exception of royal gardens, particularly those at Falkland and Stirling, any mention of gardens in old leases or household accounts is extremely rare.

Then again, gardens are seldom, if ever, mentioned by contemporary travellers. These were few and far between, and, in addition, many were biased against our country; but surely they would not have neglected to describe a good garden or a flourishing neighbourhood, if only to draw comparison between it and the general desolate condition of the country?

Lastly, we come to the diet of the country. It is universally believed that gardening in every country began with the cultivation of esculents, and only after that did the evolution of the pleasure garden commence. All commentators of Scotland, whether friendly or hostile, are loud in their denunciations of the food of the country, high and low. The only vegetable universally grown was Colewort or Kail. Onions and Peas and Beans were occasionally grown, but very rarely by the general populace until the end of the seventeenth century. Fruit was equally neglected except in monastic establishments. Is it any wonder that gardens were scarce when vegetables and fruit played such a very small part in the national diet?

It is possible that some people may have fallen into error and imagined that large gardens, as we know them, were common owing to the old meaning of the word garden. This has been dealt with later in this book, but briefly the term garden in Scotland often meant something between an allotment and a small holding. In our old system of agriculture forage crops were unknown on farmland. When the advantage of storing winter fodder for animals began slowly to be realized, Red Clover was commonly grown in the garden. When Flax and Wheat were planted, they were also often grown in the garden. On the other hand, in some parts of the country, particularly in Angus and Kincardineshire, gardens for growing vegetables, fruit and flowers were often termed yards. So mistakes may have arisen owing to terminology.

After the Restoration our gardening sense quickened in a remarkable degree. Big estates with progressive landowners, who planted and gardened on a large scale, formed nuclei for a general improvement in gardens and orchards. It is from now on that records of Scottish gardens and horticulture become more plentiful, sufficient to prove without a shadow of doubt that gardening, which has become such a national pastime, first began to feel its feet shortly after 1660. But its growth among the general population was slow. At heart we are a very conservative people and tend to look askance at new notions until somebody else has proved their lasting value. Country folk fought hard against hedges and the planting of trees. It was over fifty years after Potatoes were introduced to the country that they became popular as an article of diet, for it was imagined that their introduction was a trick on the part of the landlords to stint the poorer classes of their proper sustenance of oatmeal. The same conservative influence was at work in gardening; but spread it did, until by 1775 even the smallest cottages had their gardens.

This volume ends with the Victorian era. There

would be little sense in prolonging it, as gardening is now more or less internationalized. The rose garden, the rock garden, the wild garden, the water garden, the shrub garden; who can say that they belong to any one country or any one people? We Scots may be lucky in being able to grow some genera that fare well in our northern climate; we are equally unlucky with others. The garden flora may vary in different countries, but the essence of gardening does not. The visitor has only to look at our gardens to see that we are lucky beyond the ordinary. The old idea that Scotland is a bleak land where little grows has vanished never to return. Historically we may not have so much to show as England and one or two Continental countries, but we have our national type, the walled garden, although it is only two centuries old.

We have as keen gardeners as are to be found in any country, and the climate and the soil in which a vast number of plants flourish. What more can we want?

CHAPTER I

From the Earliest Times to the Accession of James VI

1

The State of Scotland

"THE history of the gardens of England follows step by step the history of the people. In times of peace and plenty they increased and flourished and during years of war and disturbance they suffered." Thus Mrs Cecil opened her *History of Gardening in England*.

It is unfortunate that the story of Scotland before 1600 can show few periods of peace and plenty in which gardens could flourish. Strangely enough the most peaceful time was as long ago as the century from 1174, the date of the Treaty of Falaise, to 1286, when Alexander III died. From the latter date to 1578, when James VI came to the throne, the country experienced hardly a decade of peace for close on three hundred years. It is the custom to clothe the grim years of the Middle Ages with romance. There was little enough in so-called civilized Europe; in Scotland there was none. In truth we were a barbarous nation. Occasionally we think we can detect a thin veneer of civilization on the surface, but it was a

* Superior figures refer to the list of books in the Bibliography.

veneer that would not bear the slightest scratch.

Incurable romanticists like Sir Walter Scott could write: "The garden, at first intended merely for producing esculent vegetables, fruits and flowers, began to assume another character, so soon as the increase of civilization tempted the feudal baron to step a little way out of the limits of his fortifications, and permitted his high dame to come down from her seat upon the castle walls, so regularly assigned to her by ancient minstrels, and tread with stately pace the neighbouring precincts which art had garnished for her reception". Such a gentle evolution of the garden may have taken place in England; in Scotland the feudal baron had ceased to exist before any real and general progress was possible.

England, always in closer touch with the rest of Europe, was quicker to absorb culture and peaceful pursuits. The Crown was sufficiently powerful to enforce internal peace over long periods. Above all, the country was free from invasion except in the extreme north.

Scotland, on the other hand, lay in a backwater and was out of touch with the rest of the world, so much so that all kinds of miraculous stories were in circulation in Europe during the fifteenth century. There were supposed to be floating islands on Loch Lomond, and a wonderful Pear tree, of which Pope Pius II wrote: "I had previously heard that there was a tree in Scotland, that growing on the banks of rivers produced fruits in the form of geese, which, as they approached ripeness, dropped off of their own accord".[6] Those that fell in the water flew away, those

2

that fell on land rotted. The Pope complained that whenever he asked where this astounding occurrence took place he was always told that it was further to the north.

The Crown was often incapable of enforcing internal peace. The more fertile half of the country lay next the English border and was constantly open to invasion, if not on a large scale, at least to border forays which were frequently more destructive than regular warfare.

One often hears of Scotland's close connection with France, but this was almost entirely political and the nation at large did not gain much benefit. Friendly travellers were few, while such Scots as visited the Continent were unable to take advantage on their return home of any improvements which might have affected their houses and estates.

It is little wonder that a peaceful occupation like gardening made little headway, an occupation that requires freedom of action, absence of strife and a feeling of goodwill among neighbours. Not one of these was attainable by the highest or the lowest for years at a time.

The evolution of the country house was far slower in Scotland than in England. Even in the days of James VI architecture only gradually responded to the feeling of peace and more civilized conditions. It was not until the Restoration that the country house in the lowlands really altered and ceased from being a minor fortress which could shelter dependents and herds in times of trouble. In the highlands civilization progressed much more slowly.

3

Scottish baronial architecture is usually divided into four periods. The first, in the thirteenth century, consisted of an extended system of buildings with strong and lofty walls of enceinte. This was a time more or less of external peace. The second period was the simple Norman keep, made necessary by the extreme poverty and lawlessness of the country caused by the terrible invasions of Edward I. In a few cases the keep was surrounded by walls enclosing a courtyard, but the grim, unadorned central tower was always the main line of defence. During the third period, from 1400 to 1542, the simple square keep was modified by the addition of another wing at right angles to the main building; this was called the L plan. As the population began slowly to increase, other additions crept in towards the end of this period. The fourth, from 1542 to 1700, showed the gradual influence of the Renaissance.[47] When military construction became less of a necessity, owners were not satisfied with the confined and cramped accommodation of their forebears.

It was only during the last period that the presence of many gardens was possible. Apart from any other considerations, the sites chosen for castles in the first three periods were usually such that the formation of a garden was a physical impossibility. Most of the castles were built on a small area difficult of approach and on a small scale, very different from similar structures in England.

The physical condition of the lowlands was another factor that influenced the cultivation of the soil. Much of the fine agricultural land of the present day

4

was completely useless owing to lack of drainage. Low-lying stretches, such as the Carse of Gowrie, were filled with water or were impenetrable bogs. Blau's *Atlas* shows over twenty lochs in Fife alone, many of them as large as Loch Leven, while other records prove that their number and size were not exaggerated. This stagnation of low-lying country drove tillage up the slopes to higher ground, a fact that is noted by most early travellers. Famine was common when the surface of the soil was only scratched and fodder crops were unknown.

The absence of timber was yet another evil influence. In the reign of David I, about 1125, wood was still the usual fuel throughout the country, although even then peat and moss were coming into use. In the middle of the twelfth century the great forests of the lowlands began to disappear. By the fifteenth century the vast proportion had gone and the countryside was left treeless.[7] The Crown did what it could to stop this wholesale destruction. A number of laws were passed both to promote the growing of timber and to prevent the total loss of the few trees that remained. In 1424 the Government became alarmed at the number of those who "by night steal greenwood or peal the bark of trees, destroying wood".[8] In 1447 an act was passed which ordained that all tenants should plant woods and trees, make hedges and sow Broom.[7] The frequency with which these acts were imposed shows that they were seldom obeyed, a sign that the central authority had little power in the land outside the larger towns.

Early travellers almost without exception remarked

on the bare and bleak character of the countryside. Aeneas Sylvius Piccolomini, afterwards Pope Pius II, who visited Scotland during the reign of James I, recounted how the country between Berwick and Edinburgh was destitute of trees.[8] Large areas from Berwick in the south to Angus in the north, and as far west as Stirling, must have been treeless, but wide stretches of the highlands were thickly timbered, at least until the eighteenth century. Even during the reign of Queen Mary a few outlying portions of the ancient Forest of Caledonia still existed; for instance, in Galloway, in the valley of the Dumfriesshire Esk and in the foothills of the Grampians from Edzell to Dunkeld.

Another noticeable feature that existed until the seventeenth century was the absence of enclosures to the fields. Scarcely a hedge, wall, paling or ditch was to be seen. Is it any wonder that the French attendants of Queen Mary called Scotland in disgust the *"lourde Écosse"*? It is difficult for us to visualize our country as such a barren waste. Unfortunately the evidence is so universal and overwhelming that there is no other course open but to believe it.

2

Monastic Gardens

The one exception to the general unrest was on land owned by the Church. As a rule Church property was respected, although occasionally, in particular on the Borders, monasteries were sacked and their land ravaged. Yet in comparison with the rest of the country, the monks were allowed to till their fields, orchards and gardens in peace.

It is impossible to prove or disprove Loudon's statement that a garden existed during the sixth century at the Abbey of Icolmkill in the Hebrides.[45] The Celtic Church, however, to which it belonged, paid little attention to agriculture, still less to gardens. Loudon quoted Dr. Walker's *Essays*: "On a plain adjoining the gardens of the abbey, and surrounded by small hills, there are vestiges of a large piece of artificial water, which has consisted of several acres, and been contrived both for pleasure and utility. Its banks have been formed by art into walks; and though now a bog, you may perceive the remains of a broad green terrace passing through the middle of it, which has been raised considerably above the water." That fishponds existed is probable; but that a sheet of water, walks and terraces were made for pleasure in the sixth century is quite out of the question.

As the power of the new Anglo-Norman families grew in Scotland, so did that of the Roman Church. The Romanization and Anglicization was completed by the reign of David I, about 1130, when most of the Sees were already founded. To begin with, the heads of the Church were almost entirely Anglo-Normans who brought with them knowledge of agriculture and fruit-growing gained in the large monasteries of the south. They quickly turned their attention to cultivation of the soil, and before long almost every monastery had its garden and orchard.

It is unfortunate that most of the Scottish monas-

tic records have been destroyed, but sufficient survive
to show us that many of these monastic gardens and
orchards were extensive and, for the times, well cultivated. One of the earliest records is that of the
royal gardens at Perth given by Alexander II to the
Dominican Friars on their arrival about 1230. These
gardens faced the river Tay and the North Inch and
lay adjacent to the Castle Gavel. The old Royal
Manse stood nearby and was occupied by the Friars
until their own buildings were completed. Among
these was a new guest-house, often occupied by the
kings until the capital was transferred from Perth to
Edinburgh after the murder of James I. It was from
a spacious summer-house, called the Gilten Arbour,
attached to the Priory and overlooking the North
Inch, that Robert III witnessed, on October 23, 1396,
the great fight between the clans with thirty picked
men on each side.

During one period there was also a House of the
Carthusian Order in Perth, the only one of its kind
in Scotland. Little is known about it, but probably
each choir-monk had to keep a small garden, which
was a custom of the Order.

In the *Ordinale Conventus Vallis Caulium* which
was followed by the Monasteries at Beauly, Pluscarden and Ardchattan is the following reference to
gardens, a reference which shows that all the Houses
of that Order were supposed to cultivate gardens:
"*Cantata tercia, ad refectionem conveniant ordine quo
dictum est. Post refectionem pausent in lectis suis
usque ad nonam. Post nonam ad biberes, post biberes
unusquisque in deputato sibi ortulo aut in cellula*

potest unusquisque usque ad primum signum vespere laborare". ("When tierce has been sung let them repair to the refectory in the same order. After their meal let them rest upon their beds until the office of None. After None let them go to their Collation, after Collation every one may work in the garden or cell assigned to him until the first bell for vespers.")

The size of the monasteries varied greatly, that of Melrose sometimes numbering over a hundred monks with an equal number of lay brothers, while Beauly is supposed never to have exceeded a Prior and seven monks.[4] The size and importance of the gardens consequently varied in like manner. The Tyronensian Houses were particularly famous for their well-kept gardens and orchards, those of Kilwinning, Lindores and Lesmahagow being specially mentioned in the records, while Arbroath is said to have cultivated the first Cabbages in Scotland.

The Cistercians were also great gardeners. The Abbey of Balmerino in Fife, founded in 1229 by Queen Ermengarde, widow of William the Lion, and her son Alexander II, was particularly favoured. At the time of the General Chapter of 1533 the monks asked permission to retain their private gardens, which by rule they should not have possessed. The Commissioner assented to their request so long as no monk had a larger garden than his neighbour, so long as a common way was made through all the gardens by opening a passage from one to another, and so long as the productions of the gardens were pooled in a common stock for the benefit of all the members of the House.[11]

The Monastery gardens lay east and south of St. Mary's Church. The trees were long famous in Fife. Two fine Spanish Chestnuts and a great Walnut still stood in 1793, while in 1775 Lord Hailes wrote to James Boswell: "The gentleman at St. Andrews, who said that there were but two trees in Fife, ought to have added, that the Elms of Balmerino were sold within these twenty years to make pumps for the fire-engines".

Most of the foundations were large landholders. In the records it is interesting to see how enthusiastic the Abbots and Priors were in improving their estates; indeed, without these centres of intelligent cultivation Scotland, as an agricultural country, would have sunk to an even lower level than it did.

Although quite a small monastery, the Abbey of Cupar was rich in lands. Entries dealing with gardens in outlying estates are so frequently mentioned in the Register that they prove that the Abbots and their community must have taken great care of their own gardens at the Abbey. After an act was passed by the Crown in 1457 ordaining all freeholders, temporal and spiritual, to plant on their estates trees, hedges and Broom, the authorities of the Abbey enjoined their tenants at Aberbothry to plant Ash trees and Osiers, an injunction that was continued in all the principal leases. In his lease obtained at Pentecost 1471, David Simonson, tacksman at Cupar Grange, became bound to "plant in his gardens, at least on the edge, timber, viz. ashes, sauchs, and osiers".[62] Other tenants became bound to protect the trees and hedgerows. In 1473 the tenant of Aberbothry under-

10

took to plant on each side of his farm steading a park of Broom, which was mostly used for laying on the floor of the Monastery. As a eulogy follows on the value of warrens, it is probable that its value as food and shelter for rabbits was fully recognized.

There are numerous other charters of this Abbey, such as that of the lands at Galloraw: "Charter by Donald, Abbot of Cupar, and the convent thereof giving . . . houses and gardens . . . and they shall plant orchards, herb-gardens, flower-gardens, and other things suitable to this soil".[62]

In the growing of fruit the monks excelled. Orchards (*pomaria*) were known before 1202.[14] By 1245 those belonging to the monastery of Haddington were called old, a fame which continued for several centuries—and spread far beyond Scotland. Apple and Pear trees were imported by the monks from their English and French houses, while the monks raised their own varieties as well. The famous old Apple, the Arbroath Oslin, the popularity of which lasted in Angus and Perthshire for several centuries, certainly came from the Abbey at Arbroath.[54]

Apples, and particularly Pears, were the usual fruits, although Plums were also grown. Dene Matho Tachet, a monk of Culross, sold 15 "plowm" trees to the treasurer of James IV in 1503;[63] they were probably Bullaces. Vines were grown on the orchard walls of the Border Monasteries of Melrose and Jedburgh, and even as far north as Balmerino. In addition to raising fruit trees in quantity, some monasteries must have had nurseries of forest trees and hedge plants, for an ecclesiastic, Schir John Millar, was able to supply James IV in 1497 with 1100 young trees,[14] a large number unless a nursery existed on quite an extensive scale. In the same year Don Pedro de Ayala, Ambassador from Ferdinand and Isabella of Spain, wrote: "There are all kinds of garden fruits a cold country can possess".[62] This must refer to the highly productive orchards belonging to the numerous monastic establishments.

These monastic orchards were of great importance in supplying the monks with food. Comment is frequently made by early travellers on the poor quality of the fruit, especially Pears which were grown in large quantities, but in those days a large proportion of the fruit was grown to be eaten cooked and mashed, as Turnips are to-day. The variety of vegetables was so poor and the quality so bad that anything additional which could be grown with comparative ease was of great value in a vegetarian diet.

·In many cases these orchards are known to have been of large extent. As late as 1814 an orchard of 6 or 7 acres existed which had belonged to the Abbey of Lindores in Fife. In its way it was unique, because it had been left untouched since the Reformation. In 1814 the few trees still standing were Apples and Pears. The local inhabitants recognized the poor quality of the Pears and called them "Choak Pears", "Pear Wash" and "Pear De'il". On the other hand the Apples were good and included French Rennets and Black and Grey Courpendues. A Newton Pippin (nothing to do with the American Apple of that name) is mentioned, a large green Apple with red streaks and protuberances. Honey Plums had also been grown but they had disappeared.[10]

Some orchards and gardens were surrounded by stone walls; others by hedges and ditches. Pennant in describing his visit to the Cistercian Abbey of Paisley mentioned the garden wall, "a very noble and extensive one of cut stone, conveying some idea of the antient grandeur of the place".[58] From an inscription this wall had been built in 1484 by the Abbot, George Shaw.

The monastic houses of Morayshire were equally famous for their gardens and orchards. The Priory of Pluscarden was renowned in the district, and so were the Priory of Beauly and the Abbey of Kinloss. The gardens of the two last were much improved by the arrival in 1540 of William Lubias from Dieppe, a remarkable gardener who was skilled both at planting and at grafting and who certainly benefited the whole countryside. He laid out the garden and orchard at Beauly Priory when Bishop Reid built the palace there in 1544. Mary Queen of Scots is said to have stayed in the guest-house of the Priory in 1564, and on looking out of her window on the gardens to have praised their beauty and exclaimed "*Quel beau lieu!*" In 1877 two trees, an Apple and a Pear, were still alive. The stump of the Pear was 8 feet 4 inches in circumference and the Apple 6 feet, trees of enormous size.[5] In 1450 Lord Lovat had given the monks spurs of Pears and Apples brought from the south.

The gardens of the Abbey of Kinloss were famous before Lubias arrived. William Culross, twenty-first Abbot, became so corpulent that he committed the management of the Abbey to Thomas Crystall as his

successor. It was the habit of this Abbot to do much
with his own hands. "He wrote various books of
ritual for the house, and laboured even to fatigue in
the gardens, in planting and grafting trees, and other
works of this nature." [73]

The monks took extraordinary pains over the preparation of their orchards. Towards the end of the
eighteenth century a Mr Ferguson of Pitfour in
Aberdeenshire uncovered the remains of an ancient
pomarium belonging to the Abbey of Deer, while
preparing ground for a new orchard. On the top was
a three-foot layer of rich soil; then a paved causeway.
Beneath was a bed of sand and then another paved
causeway.[54] Other records also describe this method
of planting, which was generally practised. These
elaborate preparations must have been carried out
partly to secure efficient drainage and partly to prevent the tap roots from penetrating too deep into
the soil.

In abbeys and priories all the inmates from the
abbot to the lay brothers and the tenants laboured in
the gardens and orchards. Some of the Bishops, on
the other hand, employed professional gardeners.
The Bishopric of Dunkeld was an important See in
the fifteenth and sixteenth centuries. The actual site
of the ancient monastery was occupied in 1505 by
the east garden of the Bishop's palace; in addition, he
had another garden at Cluny, a few miles to the east.
During the period covered by the *Rentale Dunkeldense*,[25] from 1505 to 1517, three gardeners are mentioned: John Leslie from 1506 to 1509; John Brown,
who appeared to have worked principally at Cluny,

14

from about 1508 to 1510; and Robert Howyson. It is odd that very few items deal with the garden other than the wages of the gardeners, yet the Bishop lived well and even in luxury for the times; dried figs, pepper, cinnamon and sugar are mentioned in the accounts.

There is no item for fruit trees, but these may have been obtained from the Abbey of Cupar. One pound of Beans was purchased for 12s. 4d. (Scots) and sent "to Clony and sown there". Vegetable seeds are included several times, principally Onions and Cabbage, but in small quantities for so large an establishment. Flowers are never mentioned, but there must have been secluded gardens, rectangular areas of grass surrounded with walls and shaded by trees.

The most detailed information to be gained, and that is only of subsidiary interest, is that dealing with gardeners' wages. These were of two types, a fixed amount of victual and a sum per annum in money amounting to 75 pounds (Scots). The victual wage may only have meant free board, because during the absence of the Bishop the gardeners sometimes received in lieu a further 4d. a day of what might be termed board wages. One under-gardener is mentioned, "Lesleis Jok", who received a mere pittance of a peck of meal a week. Thirty or forty years later gardeners were also found in clothes and "schoon".

It is quite impossible at this distance to have any clear idea of what was grown in monastic gardens. We know of a few plants, but no identifiable list of a garden flora exists until a much later date. The Hop has been found wild at Lindores Abbey, possibly an escape from the monastic garden: a very strong tradition believes that *Tulipa sylvestris*, which used to be found in quantity in the woods about Balmerino Abbey, was first introduced by the monks. Other plants which are not indigenous are found near the precincts of old monasteries, such as the common Wallflower, the Musk Mallow (*Malva moschata*), the Sweet Violet, and various Stonecrops and House-leeks, for example, *Sedum reflexum* and *Sempervivum tectorum*.

The Herb Garden was more important, for the monks physicked not only their own tenants but the whole countryside. There were found the herbs from which were made their simples and tisanes and clysters; Elecampane for coughs and stomach, Tansy a cure for the gout, Barberry as a febrifuge, St. John's Wort for hysteria, and so on. It was for their medicinal value, supposed or genuine, that exotic plants were usually brought into this country from abroad in monastic times; that they may have been good to look upon or have smelt sweetly was a secondary consideration.

Some herbs were doubtless handed down from the pre-Christian era through the monasteries of the Celtic Church, such as *Menyanthes trifoliata*, the Buckbean, in the opinion of some authorities the original Shamrock. The root was eaten as a vegetable by the Celts, who considered it to be a panacea for all ills and particularly valuable in reducing fever. In monasteries of the Celtic Church both in Ireland and on the west of Scotland, such as Iona, special boggy pools had been made for its cultivation.

16

3

Castle Gardens

It is much more difficult to trace the growth of lay, as opposed to monastic, gardens. The gradual infiltration into the country of the great Anglo-Norman families in the twelfth century must have brought with it something of Norman culture, but whether this could survive the lean times of the fourteenth and fifteenth centuries is another matter. Crude though our civilization was, it could not remain completely blind to the obvious advantages of orchards and gardens which could be seen in the numerous monastic foundations scattered throughout the more fertile areas. Nevertheless if the monk was a good teacher, it is doubtful if the general populace was an apt pupil. If it had been, the lower and middle classes could not, by any stretch of the imagination, have remained so satisfied with the universal diet of meal and kail which persisted until the eighteenth century was well advanced. We are told over and over again that the reputation of the climate was such that it was impossible to grow trees and many vegetables, but it is difficult to believe that no one had sufficient imagination, with the example of the monasteries before him, to experiment for himself.

It is probable that before the latter half of the fifteenth century lay gardens were few in number. The people as a whole were accustomed to pass their lives in a rut. Up to a few generations ago we were notoriously conservative in our method of living, and this conservatism undoubtedly has existed for many centuries. Apart from any trait in character the times were against any sustained growth of peaceful pursuits. During the first three periods of Scottish architecture the primary value of the dwelling-house was as a place of possible safety in times of trouble. Inside the castle walls it was most unlikely that space which could be utilized as a sanctuary for the owner's herds would be filled with fruit trees or garden crops; while outside the walls no orchards or gardens which might hide the approach of raiders were allowed in the immediate foreground. In addition, the sites and architectural features of many castles did not allow space for garden or orchard. Thus, even with the example of the monasteries before the people, one is forced to the conclusion that large gardens were very rare before 1450.

After that date they appear to have increased, at any rate in areas that were under direct control of the Crown, for Chalmers states that gardens were universal in Midlothian during the reign of James III, from 1460 to 1488.[14] Unfortunately family records of this period are so scarce that it is impossible to learn details. Later even foreigners attending Queen Mary's court tempered their scorn of our countryside by remarking that noblemen's seats in Lothian were "beautified with fair orchards and gardens".[8] It is possible to find occasional references elsewhere, but almost invariably no details are given: for instance, Cherry orchards existed at Ballencrief in Midlothian as long ago as 1514,[64] but it is quite impossible to discover the size, age or quality of the trees.

18

The one exception to the general dearth of early gardens appears to have been those attached to the royal castles. From the accession of David I in 1124 to the death of Alexander III in 1286 castles held by the Crown increased in number throughout the country and were used to hold the country in obedience. We can learn from the records that many of them had gardens. During the reign of David I there was one at the base of the Castle Rock in Edinburgh and others attached to the royal castles of Roxburgh and Jedburgh. David II must have continued the Edinburgh garden, as a charter exists granting the keeping of the King's Garden to a Malcolm Pagainson.[14] We hear of another royal garden attached to the Castle of Elgin in 1261 when Robert Spink, a crossbowman, claimed the garden in right of his wife, as her ancestors had held it as a hereditary right on condition that the King was supplied with Kail and Garlic when he was in residence, a method of tenure that was commonly practised. This was during a period of comparative tranquillity which ended at the death of Alexander III. From 1286 to about 1450 little is recorded of even Royal Gardens.

By far the most important garden prior to 1600 was that of the Royal Castle of Stirling. Just sufficient is known to whet our appetite for more. It was one of the few of its time to conform with our idea of a garden; where herbs, vegetables, flowers and fruit were grown, and where a portion of it, at any rate, was laid out solely for pleasure.

Even before 1450 a small area on the top of the Castle Rock had been set aside as a garden. It was probably no more than a square of turf between the walls where the ladies of the court could spend an occasional hour of peace, but it was definitely called a garden.

Later James III made a new garden on sloping ground by the Round Table, an ancient place of tribal assembly below the Castle Rock. This was enlarged by James IV about 1496 so as to include not only the mound of the Round Table but also the surrounding meadows. Close by was a small natural loch from which water was drawn for ponds and canals among the flower beds to make what must have been one of the first ornamental gardens in Scotland.

From the dry bones of the Exchequer Rolls and the Accounts of the Lord High Treasurer we can learn something about the garden but not very much; unfortunately no plan exists which could help us to reconstruct its exact appearance. From above the skeleton of a garden can still be made out among the fields, but this is of a later date. When the new garden was made, it was apparently placed under the charge of James Wilson, who was responsible from about 1460 to 1470 for keeping the parks and lawns of the older Palace of Falkland. One can judge from the accounts that Wilson was more of a general factotum than a skilled gardener. In addition to keeping the parks and lawns he was constantly at work cleaning out ditches and building walls.[64]

By 1479, however, Stirling must have been sufficiently important to have been separated from Falkland, as Gilles Margilhoise and Malcolm Mackley were drawing regular wages for looking after the garden. Possibly they were little use, for in 1484 we find John Modane in charge of both Falkland and Stirling under the terms of no fruit and vegetables no pay, a kind of wage contract which obviously proved satisfactory as it occurs several times. In 1495 John Gardinar, the gardener at Falkland, had to supply eight barrels of Onions before his wages were paid: in 1496 these were withheld as he failed to supply the requisite quantity.[64]

It seems probable that hired labour of the professional gardener type was unsatisfactory at this early date. At least twice, in 1494 and again in 1497, two monks, Archibald Hamilton and Robert Caldwell, were called in to repair and help in the King's garden. Even this cannot have been sufficient, for in 1497 extensive alterations were started under the superintendence of Schir John Scharp, the King's Chaplain. By 1499 the garden was reported to be in good condition and by 1502 the new "great garden" was completed. The chaplain must have been a man of some attainment in gardening, as he also laid out the gardens at Holyrood.[63]

Money had been spent in draining and in "castin of dikis". There are quite a number of entries recording the purchase of seeds, particularly Onions, Leeks and Kail. In 1498 the sum of 18s. was allowed to "by peis and berrys with". There was at least one purchase of Thorns; in 1501 400 were bought for 21s., a very early date for hedges except on monastic lands. Fruit trees were also supplied, the "plowm" trees by Dene Matho Tachet of Culross mentioned before, and 15 Pear trees by Phipson in the Canongate in Edinburgh, who also supplied Willows. Vines were also grown. Strawberries were not known in gardens at that date, but the King obviously liked wild berries which were constantly brought in and paid for.[63]

Some attempt was also made to furnish the herb garden. Collectors were sent out through the neighbouring districts to bring in the requisite herbs.[14] In February 1501 the gardener at Scone was sent to Perth with plants and trees for the King. These were dispatched to Stirling a few days later in nine horse loads.

After Flodden the garden was neglected, but we hear of it again being kept up in 1530 by James V. This must have been the most interesting period, if only there were records, because the King had spent several years at the French court and was certainly imbued with the spirit of the Renaissance. He brought over a French gardener, Bartrand Gallôtre, to take charge of Stirling with three gardeners under him.[63]

During the reign of Queen Mary the garden was also kept in condition. In 1563 a sum was allowed for repairs of dykes, ditches and ponds. Shortly after Stirling was given up as a royal residence, but the garden still continued, for accounts of 1629 show that wages were paid to William Waltir "Maister Gairdner to his Majestie at the Castell of Stirling".

Defoe visited the site about 1720; accustomed as he was to the more stilted style of the formal garden, his comments are interesting. He wrote: "In the park, adjoining the Castle were formerly large gardens,

how fine they were I cannot say; the figure of the walks and grass-plats remains plain to be seen, they are very old fashion'd; but I suppose the gardens might be thought fine, as gardens were then; particularly they had not then the usage of adorning their gardens with evergreens, trimm'd and shap'd; trees espalier'd into hedges and such-like, as now: they had, indeed, statues and busts, Vasa and fountains, flowers and fruit; but we make gardens fine now many ways, which those ages had no genius for; as by scrouls, embroidery, pavillions, terrases, and slopes, pyramids and high espaliers, and a thousand ornaments, which they had no notion of".[21] The remains which he mentions are probably those of 1629 or thereabouts.

At such a distance of time and with so little pattern on which to work, it would be idle to try and reconstruct what this Stirling Castle garden looked like. We can only suppose that it cannot, at any rate during the reign of James V, have differed greatly from a Tudor garden in the north of England. There were probably railed beds with Pansies and Cowslips, Marigolds and Bachelors' Buttons, Cornflowers and Hollyhocks. There might possibly have been dry earth-banks, popular at the time in North of England gardens, with Wallflowers planted on the top.

In 1507 a garden was made on the site of the drained loch at the Abbey of Holyrood House from the designs of Schir John Scharp, the King's chaplain. Fees were paid to him for several years to keep it in order.[63] Perhaps this is the same garden that

is shown in an existing drawing of a portion of
Edinburgh, including Holyrood, which, it is believed,
was prepared by spies to aid the Earl of Hertford's
expedition of 1544.[3] It is a kind of bird's-eye plan
which distinctly shows three walled enclosures with
sketchy outlines of trees, obviously meant to be
gardens. The gardens of Holyrood always seem to
have been of secondary importance and to have been
improved spasmodically. In the seventeenth century
at least one portion was let as a market garden, while
another, called St. Ann's Yards, became in 1670 the
first home of the Physick Garden.

4

Town and Village Gardens

When dealing with town and village gardens we
come across the difficulty of defining the word garden. Although the term garden is often met with,
it applied more to a small holding than to what we
recognize as a garden. There were several reasons for
this apparent anomaly. The areas covered by most
towns and villages were large for the number of
houses and the size of their population. Houses were
scattered and almost invariably had plots of land
attached which were too large for the small amount
of vegetables used in the everyday diet of the poorer
classes. The usual vegetables were Kail and Cabbage,
and, to a lesser extent, Peas and Beans. Thus Bere
for their pot barley and Oats for their meal were
often grown in these garden plots.

As early as 1269 tithes of gardens in cities and boroughs were paid to the bishop, and in villages to the parson if corn was grown in them; if no corn was grown, the tithes were paid to the bishop.[14] It is surprising at what a late date houses in even the more thickly populated portions of cities still possessed their attached gardens. In 1603 tenements in the Cowgate in Edinburgh had their own plots, and in Leith certainly as late as 1609.[14]

Fruit was never grown in these gardens owing to the vicious system of short leases which were often limited to one year, sometimes to three years in the case of farms, but never to more than five years. This at once negatived any idea of improving the land, because the tenant knew that at the end of his lease he would either have to pay an increased rent or be turned out if there were visible and open signs of improvement.

As a rule, towns were more backward than the countryside. Even in the reign of Queen Mary they were still in the condition of the Middle Ages, when it was the first duty of every good citizen to take his place as a man-at-arms in the defence of his town. Jealousy between towns was rife, and trading was strictly limited to the burghers' own town except during the annual fairs. In addition, towns had large suburban areas allotted to them, whose inhabitants were forbidden to trade in any other market.[8] This restriction was particularly irksome with its attendant system of an "intrinsic just price", a system evolved to prevent townsmen from having to pay too high prices in the market. These were fixed from time to time by an appointed body of townsmen, and were only settled when the goods were actually on sale. This may have helped the consumer, but it destroyed any idea of improvement whether in trading, agriculture or gardening, as cost and the law of supply and demand were not allowed to be taken into account.

There was no incentive to improve either the quantity or the quality of market produce, as the farmer or gardener never knew whether he would make a profit or a loss until the goods were actually on sale. That system of the "intrinsic just price" was undoubtedly one of the reasons why Scotland lagged so far behind in agriculture and gardening. With a small population and trade of all kinds hedged in by so many rules and regulations, there was little use in a man producing more foodstuffs than he and his family could eat. It certainly delayed the formation of market gardens in Scotland for many years after they were well established in England. If the populace would not eat vegetables, there was no point in growing them; and the poorer classes in town and country were satisfied for many generations with their interminable kail and brose.

By the time Queen Mary came to the throne some of the great families possessed town houses in Edinburgh, Glasgow, Dundee or Aberdeen, most of them with an attached *viridarium* or garden. Usually these were only squares of grass between walls, as, for instance, in the case of the *viridarium* of the town house of the Lindsays which lay between the Nethergate and the river Tay in Dundee.[41] Occasionally, however, they were more elaborate. In the middle of the sixteenth century the Regent Moray owned a garden in Edinburgh which must have been quite extensive. It was still in existence in 1819 with some venerable Pear trees, an old weeping Thorn and the remains of Elm bowers.

In Glasgow there was what almost amounted to a miniature garden city, for nearby the Cathedral was the stately Bishop's Palace and the houses of thirty-two prebends, each one of which was surrounded by its own orchard and garden.[8]

CHAPTER II

The Start of the Country House

In the sixteenth century there appear the first signs
of improvement in the conditions of life of the
Scottish people. Some of the laws passed during the
reign of James V showed this awakening. Although
they dealt with the usual subjects of land improvement and planting, yet they were sufficiently explicit
to prove that some attention was being paid to them.

An ordinance of 1535 laid down that everyone
possessed of land worth a hundred pounds (Scots)
had to plant woods or orchards round the house. The
proprietor also had to compel his tenants to plant
one tree for every merk-land which they held of him.[8]
In a royal rental book of 1541 of what must have been
a model estate strict conditions were laid down for
tenants. Each tenant had to have near his house a
large well-furnished garden, hedged with Thorn,
Willow, Alder or Aspen. For every acre of land for
which he paid a silver merk he had to plant three
trees, Ash, Plane or Elm; for every chalder of Wheat
or Barley reaped twenty trees, for every chalder of
Oats ten trees. A superior class of tenant had to
possess an "honest mansion" with an orchard or
garden carefully fenced or surrounded with trees.[8]

Such conditions were obeyed by the richer classes, but it is very doubtful if poorer tenants paid any attention to them, so imbued were they with the belief that trees round a field were more of a curse than a blessing. Even as late as the eighteenth century many farmers said that tree roots stole nourishment from soil meant for crops, that grain on the shady side of the field never ripened, and that trees encouraged a host of birds which devoured the grain in the ear.

It is from now on that travellers' accounts differed. They were still in agreement that there were no large woods or forests in central and eastern lowland Scotland; but some, who may have gained their information second or third hand, still repeat the common complaint of a completely treeless land. John Major in his *History of Greater Britain* wrote: "Neither do they plant trees or hedges for their orchards, nor do they dung the land: and this is no small loss and damage to the whole realm". On the other hand, Fynes Moryson, who was a confessed globe-trotter and was usually accurate in his statements, is more guarded. He has been misquoted, or rather half-quoted, which alters his meaning completely. He wrote in 1598 of Fife: "This Countrey is populous and full of Noblemens and Gentlemens dwellings commonly compassed with little groves, though trees are so rare in these parts, as I remember not to have seen one wood". This surely proved that trees for shelter had already been planted for several years.

New varieties of fruit trees and of vegetables and flowers filtered into the country, but unfortunately efforts in this direction were partly negatived by the bad cultivation which was usually practised. Tillage in the fields was not improved by the vicious system of run-rigging, a method which was also followed in gardens. Cattle, horse or pig manure was unknown until a later date, as stock was grazed on common land the year round. Near the coast seaweed was used as a fertilizer, but unless it was spread as soon as collected it rotted and lost its value.

One of the reasons against the more rapid growth of gardens before the seventeenth century appears to have been the lack of a class of professional gardeners. Probably this lack was partly owing to the ignorance that such a class was a necessity if gardens were to flourish, but it was mostly due to the general poverty of the country and the impossibility of paying sufficient to attract a good type of working man. Professional gardeners who were paid a salary were few, but a number of records exist of contracts between landlord and gardener whereby the latter was allowed to work a portion of the land for his own benefit in return for his labour. As an example, there was a contract between Alexander Dunbar, Dean of Moray, and his gardeners, dated November 7, 1566, in which they shall "labor the gryt orcheart and gardeings of the said Dene's manss within the channonrie of Elgin" for which they shall have "the taill at the end of the orcheart to be usit by thaim to their utelitie and profeit".[24] As late as 1723 James Ramsay, gardener at Gordonstoun in Moray, was only paid 150 pounds (Scots) per annum with free house.

Perhaps where foreigners worked, like Gallôtre at Stirling or Lubias at Beauly Priory, small centres of better cultivation existed from which knowledge slowly spread through the neighbourhood; but the general level of cultivation was very poor until after the Restoration.

One or two districts or individual gardens are picked out by historians and travellers for special comment. Linlithgow and Lothian generally were in advance of the rest of the country. Among the most often quoted was Seton Castle, possibly because it lay close to one of the highroads from England to Edinburgh and so was much in the public eye. Centuries ago Sir Richard Maitland wrote that in 1560 "this Lord biggit ane grit dyk and wall of stane about the yarde and grit orcheart of Seytoun; and also biggit ane pretty hous upon the gardin syd thairof".[50] Still later, in 1636, Sir William Brereton wrote of it: "Here also are apple-trees, walnut-trees, sycamore and other fruit-trees, and other kinds of wood which prosper well". Seton Castle was pulled down in 1790.

Moray was particularly favoured in the middle of the sixteenth century. Bishop Leslie described it as "a country without alane by all the rest commendet with ws for baith plentie and pleisure, for it is eivin and plane, without dubis and myres, mervellous delectable in fair forrests, in thik wodis, in sueit sairing flowris, weil smelling herbis, pleisant medowis, fine quheit, and al kynde of stuffe orchardes and fruitful gairdings, and them sa neir the coste".[8] The monastic records of Beauly, Pluscarden and Kinloss also bear

31

witness to the fruitful state of Moray during the sixteenth century.

One of the earliest extant pleasure gardens is that attached to the castle of Edzell in Kincardineshire. It is unfortunate that only the walls and the garden house are standing. Flower-beds there must have been, but no trace of them survives; nor do we know what flowers were cultivated. At the end of the sixteenth century Edzell Castle was enlarged by the ninth Earl Crawford in conformity with the times. The garden we owe to his son, Sir David Lindsay, to whom is really due the credit, usually given to the second Earl of Haddington almost a century later, of being the "Father of Planting" in Scotland. At Edzell Sir David had what must have been one of the first tree nurseries in Scotland. He wrote to his half-brother, Lord Ogilvie, "your thousand young birks shall be right welcome". Lord Menmuir wrote to Sir David to remember his "firs and hollins", and promised him a supply of Elm seed.[41]

The garden at Edzell was made in 1604 to the south of the new courtyard built by his father a year or two before. It is a rectangular enclosure surrounded by a high stone wall with a garden house at the south-east corner and bathing-rooms, of which only the foundations remain, at the south-west corner. The garden is 173 feet long by 144 feet wide, enclosed on three sides by a decorated wall; the fourth, or north, side is formed by the south wall of the courtyard. "Each side is divided into compartments 10 to 11 feet wide, separated by what appear to have been square shafts. The bases, caps and

FIG. III.—THE GARDEN HOUSE AND A PART OF THE GARDEN WALL AT EDZELL CASTLE, ORIGINALLY BUILT IN 1604

central bands remain, but the shafts are gone. The compartments are arranged in two alternating designs, one containing a single recess for flowers, 3 feet wide and 2 feet 6 inches high, with a carved bas-relief above, and the other containing three rows of small recesses (about 16 inches square) arranged chequerwise with three stars above pierced in the centre as shot-holes. Over the centre of each compartment there is a small niche with a carved cushion, on which a bust or other ornament might rest. Over the niches is a small curved pediment containing a scroll. All the above-mentioned recesses have the sill hollowed out as if for the reception of soil for a flower or a plant. It is supposed that the chequered design and the three stars represent those figures in the Lindsay arms, which are gules, a fesse chequé argent and azure, with three stars in chief of the second."[47]

The bas-reliefs are twenty in number, seven on the west wide representing the Cardinal Virtues, six on the south side the Liberal Arts and seven on the east side the Planetary Deities. It has been suggested that Sir David Lindsay was given the idea by a German, Hans Ziegler, whom he brought over as a mining engineer in the hopes that a metal industry could be started in the hills behind Edzell.[65] Ziegler may have brought with him some books of engravings of George Pencz or Dürer. Sculpture, however, was not uncommon in Scotland in the early seventeenth century; it was usually crudely executed and almost always copied from elsewhere.

Edzell Castle has lately been taken over by H.M. Office of Works who have reconditioned the garden.

Flower-beds have been made and planted with common garden flowers in mauve, blue and white. The turf is kept cut, while the recesses in the walls are filled with Lobelia, which may not be in keeping with the date of the garden but looks very charming. So delightful is the appearance of this old walled garden with the blue shining from the weathered red stone of the walls that no one can imagine anyone living there without planting something in these recesses, although doubts have been cast on this explanation of their inclusion in the design.

This type of garden was not uncommon in Scottish castles of the time of Queen Mary and James VI, but there is none other so well preserved or with such excellent architectural features.

Shortly after the accession of James VI to the throne of England in 1603 there commenced a further broadening in the style of domestic architecture in the lowlands, away from the stronghold towards the mansion-house, while sites were chosen for other reasons than those of defence. As the fear of raids decreased, there was no further need of the complete lack of all cover near the dwelling-house by which enemies could approach unseen. When new houses were built, designs were made at the same time for pleasure gardens, while some of the amenities of civilization were constantly being added to old castles. In the highlands and in the valleys of the Borders the old system continued for several more generations; indeed, the latter had become so accustomed to the constant bickerings of Border feuds that it was not until the eighteenth century that the inhabitants shook off their old fears and ceased to live in the Border keeps, where lack of space forced the lord and his lady to bed down in the living-room at night.

We are so accustomed to read in contemporary accounts of the abysmal state of the Scottish countryside with its lack of timber and absence of all enclosures that we are apt to regard such a state of affairs as applicable to the whole country. Yet in some areas it was not so black as most travellers would have us believe.

Although planting in bulk was not started until after the Restoration, trees, usually hardwoods, for protection were growing round most of the larger houses early in the seventeenth century. Orchards on a larger scale were also planted, particularly in Clydeside and Midlothian. The improvement was general among landowners and not confined solely to the houses of the great. One of the Lowthers has left an interesting account of a journey he made with a friend from Cumberland to Edinburgh. He was enthusiastic about the countryside and was surprised at seeing such good cultivation, including the liming of the fields; yet one reads that liming was not practised until the eighteenth century.[34]

Lowther recorded how he visited at Gala House in Selkirkshire Sir James Pringle, a model landlord who took a great interest in trees. "He suffered his tenants to hold on him by planting 6 fruit trees or 12 other trees, and if they fail, to pay for every tree not planted 4d." Lowther then went on to describe the estate: "He hath a very pretty park, with many natural walks in it, artificial ponds and arbours now a

making, he hath neat gardens and orchards, and all
his tenants through his care, he hath abundance of
cherry trees, bearing a black cherry, some of which I
see to be about 30 yards high and a fathom thick,
great store of sycamores, trees he calleth silk trees,
and fir trees".[46]

From the insistence on planting by tenants one
can judge how difficult it was even at this date to
persuade the poorer classes to plant trees.

Closer to Edinburgh and Glasgow the countryside
must have been comparatively settled before the
close of the sixteenth century. We are told how the
Earl of Winton in 1620 "built the house of Wintone.
He founded and built the great house from the foundation with all the large stone dykes about the
precinct, park, orchard and gardens thereof."[50] No
one in their senses would have pulled down newly
built walls; so old Winton House must have been
surrounded by enclosures many years before 1620. A
hundred years later the estates, forfeited after the '15,
were bought by the York Building Company who let
them on lease to a market-gardener.

It has been stated on more than one occasion that
the old Dutch garden with its topiary work at Barncluith on the outskirts of Hamilton was first made in
1583. This is possibly placing the date too early. Evergreens were occasionally planted in gardens before
1600, but exaggerated topiary work, such as existed
at Barncluith, did not become fashionable until after
the Restoration.

Most of the gardens built during this period were
so designed as to form an architectural appendage to

FIG. IV.—THE HANGING GARDENS OF BARNCLUITH

the dwelling-house. They usually lay directly under one of the sides of the house and were surrounded by stone walls with banqueting-houses or garden shelters built at the corners. A typical example was Dundas Castle, where in 1623 Sir Walter Dundas built a parterre enclosed in walls of hewn stone with a banqueting-house at each corner. This garden was remarkable for a magnificent Renaissance sundial and fountain which stood in the middle of the parterre. The great mass of the surface carving was in low relief with elaborate masks at intervals.[47]

It is a pity that at this distance of time it is impossible to state definitely that such and such a garden was made at a particular date. It is customary to place the formation of the magnificent gardens at Drummond Castle near Crieff about the year 1630. Pleasant though it would be to look back on the unbroken existence during three centuries of more than ten acres of such a regal formal garden, yet the evidence so far produced is too slight for any such definite statement.

It rests mostly on the existence of a famous sundial and on the known character of the second Earl of Perth, "a nobleman of learning, probity and integrity, of unshaken loyalty to the King, benevolent to his friends, prudent, and economical in the management of his affairs, and just in all his dealings".[23] He is known to have been a great improver of his estates, and he certainly made a garden; but at that period when great formal gardens were unknown in Scotland he would not have been "economical in the management of his affairs", if he had suddenly started to make a formal garden about five times the size of any other north of the border. The parterres are certainly not Victorian in their design, nor are they early seventeenth century, when they were constructed on much more of a stereotyped geometrical pattern.

The famous multiplex sundial is dated 1630 and was made for the Earl by his architect, John Mylne.

The main parterre is made in the form of a St. Andrew's Cross. It is probably safe to say that, although additions and minor alterations may have been made, the original design has not been greatly changed, partly owing to the great cost of such alterations and partly because the traditions of fine parterres and the general system of planting such as this were usually followed from generation to generation. Great use had been made of edgings of Yew and Box and also of trained and clipped evergreens. This would place its formation in the period following the Restoration, somewhere about 1680, when John Reid wrote his book, *The Scots Gard'ner*. In his book Reid laid down clearly how pleasure grounds should be divided into plots by walks with a "bordure" round each plot and an evergreen trimmed in pyramidal fashion at each corner.[61]

It is unfortunate but understandable that there are so few contemporary and eighteenth-century accounts of Drummond Castle. The family was always in trouble: the fourth earl was a great adherent of James II and died in exile, while the fifth and sixth earls were staunch Jacobites and took part in the '15 and the '45. After the latter the estates were forfeited until 1784 when a collateral descendant obtained possession. Thus it was most unlikely that the garden was made between 1688 and 1784. In the absence of any definite information it would appear probable that a fine garden, and probably the terraces, were made about 1630, that it was enlarged and laid out in the design of the St. Andrew's Cross about 1670 to 1680, and that it was again enlarged towards the end of the eighteenth century.

It is known that a garden in the Dutch manner was in existence at Ormiston in 1636. This may have been made by Sir George Touris, great-grandfather of John Cockburn, the well-known "improver" of the eighteenth century. The garden was laid out in an oblong square with grass walks and interior divisions formed by hedges of Holly and Yew. There was also a bowling-green and a fine orchard.

The same process of civilization was taking place in Moray and near the coasts of the north-eastern seaboard. Sir Robert Gordon of Straloch, cartographer to Charles I, was much struck by the beauty of Dunrobin: "Dunrobin, the Erle of Sutherland his speciall residence, a house well seated upon a mote hard by the sea, with fair orchards, where there be pleasant gardens planted with all kinds of froots, hearbs and floors used in this kingdom, and abundance of good saphorn, and rosemarie, the froot being excellent, and cheeflie the pears and cherries".[33]

Towards the end of the reign of Charles I and during the Commonwealth there was little opportunity for improving estates or making gardens. There were some people, however, who for various reasons, political or otherwise, deliberately withdrew themselves and their families from all public life and lived quietly on their estates. Luckily in the *Denham Memoir* [18] we have a very complete description of an ordinary country house of 1654. This was the estate of Coltness in Lanarkshire given to Mr Thomas Stewart on his marriage by his father, Sir James Stewart of Kirkfield.

"It was agreed that, upon the marriage, the young folks should take up family in the country, and Cultness to be the place of residence. Mr Stewart applied himself to country affairs, and both husband and wife to their proper work in a retired life, and were full of beneficiency and Christian charity.

"He sett himself to planting and inclosing, and so to embellish the place. But as the old mansion-house was straitening, and their family to incress, he thought of adding to the old toure (which consisted only of a vault, and two rooms, one above the other, with a small room on top of the turnpike stair, and a garret) a large addition on south side of the staircase, of a good kitchen, celler, meat-room or low parlor, a large hall or dyning-room, with a small bed-chamber and closet over these, and above that, two bed-chambers with closets. The office-houses of bake-house, brew-house, garner-room, and men-servant's bed-chamber, were on the north of a paved court; and a high front wall toward the east, with ane arched entry or porch, inclosed all. Without this arched gaite was another larger court, with stabells on the south syde for the family and strangers' horses, and a trained up thorn with a boure in it. Opposite to the

40

FIG. V.—THE MULTIPLEX SUNDIAL AND PART OF THE FORMAL GARDEN AT DRUMMOND CASTLE

stables north from the mansion-house, with ane entry
from the small paved inner court, was a large coal-
fold, and threw it a back entry to a good spring
draw-well, as also leading to the byer, sheep-house,
barn and hen-house; all of which make a court, to the
north of the other court, and separate from it with a
stone wall, and on the east parte of this court was a
large space for a dunghill. The gardens were to the
south of the house, much improven and inlarged, and
the nursery-garden was a small square inclosure to
the west of the house. The slope of the grounds to
the west made the south garden, next the house, fall
into three cross tarrasses. The tarras fronting the
south of the house was a square parterre, or flour-
garden, and the easter and wester, or the higher and
lower plots of ground, were for cherry and nut gardens, and walnut and chestnut-trees planted upon
the head of the upper bank, towards the parterre,
and the slope bank on the east syde the parterre was
a strawberry border.

"These three tarrasses had a high stone wall on the
south, for ripening and improving finer fruits, and to
the south of this wall was a good orchard and kitchen
garden, with broad grass walks, all inclosed with a
good thorn hedge; and without this a ditch and dry
fence, inclosing severall rows of timber trees for
shelter; to the west of the house, and beyond the
square nursery-garden, was a large square timber
tree park, with birches, towards the house, and on
the other three sydes, rowes of ash and plain, and in
the middle a goodly thicket of firs. To the north of
the barn court, and north from the house, was a grass

inclosure of four akers, with a fish pond in the corner for pikes and perches. All was inclosed with a strong wall and hedge-rowes of trees: so the wholl of this policy might consist of ane oblong square, of seven or eight akers of ground, and the house near midle of the square, and the longer syde of the square fronted to the south; the ordinary entries to the house were from east and west, but the main access from the east."

This is an excellent description of a small dwelling-house, originally built for defence, which was later made comfortable. It is also one of the few contemporary accounts before 1700 of the formation of a garden and its immediate surroundings, what are called in Scotland policies. Owing to circumstances all improvements in this case were carried out in a few years, but the description shows what was being carried out on many estates through the length and breadth of Scotland, beginning slowly in the seventeenth and increasing in the eighteenth centuries.

CHAPTER III

The Age of the Formal Garden

1

The Start of Planting

IT is one of the paradoxes of Scottish history to find
that some of our greatest gardens were planned and
made during a time of acute national poverty. With
the Restoration the Crown ceased to take much
personal interest in its original Scottish patrimony.
The country was neglected, a neglect that increased
rather than diminished with the Union of the two
kingdoms. Matters were not improved by a series of
bad harvests from 1696 to 1702, and agriculture had
not recovered sufficiently to provide reserves for the
terrible year of 1709 when famine swept the country.

Yet we hear of broad plantations springing up and
great gardens in the making, of Yester and Hatton,
of Dalkeith and Leslie; but these all belonged to
peers with broad acres and, for the times, fat incomes.
There is less to be learned about smaller gardens
during this period, so little that we must conclude
that for the first fifty years after the Restoration the
small country laird with an average patrimony, still
less the man with only a few acres, could not afford
the luxury of a pleasure garden. Even before the

famine years a laird was counted well off if he had an income of £300 sterling, and of this at least half, and often two-thirds or more, was paid in kind. He could not be expected to imitate the elaborate formal garden of the Restoration with its parterres and statuary, its garden houses and water-works. Most of the wealth of the country was in cities or in the hands of a few great families.

Important though some of these formal gardens were, it would be illogical to consider them a sign of an awakening national spirit of gardening. Their entire conception was foreign to the country; where their remains exist they are not in keeping with the domestic type of garden which began to be evolved towards the middle of the eighteenth century.

Thomas Morer, who was not ill-disposed towards Scotland, was disappointed at what could be seen in 1689. He wrote: "Their avenues are very indifferent, and they want their gardens, which are the beauty and pride of our English seats".[52]

The one great advance during this period was the more general use of trees. The entire life of the lowlands and the face of the countryside was so altered during the next two centuries by intensive planting that its influence must be stressed. Fine trees have become an integral part of the policies, or immediate surroundings of the house; and the policies, garden and mansion-house have in course of time been welded into such an harmonious unit that the absence of trees is to most of us quite inconceivable.

That was not the case at the end of the seventeenth century. It is true that trees began to be used for shelter a little before 1600, but until 1700 most travellers still comment on the lack of woods in the lowlands. Some did not bother to travel far off the main roads; others, like the splenetic Thomas Kirke, so obviously belonged to the anti-Scottish faction as to be quite unreliable. Kirke wrote: "Woods they have none, that suits not with the frugality of the people, who are so far from propagating any, that they destroy those they had, upon the politick maxim, that corn will not grow in the land pestered with its roots". Though one may be amused by such scurrilities, it is difficult to take seriously the remarks of a man who could write: "The thistle was wisely placed there, partly to show the fertility of the country; nature alone producing plenty of these gay flowers, and partly as an emblem of the people, the top thereof having some colour of a flower, but the bulk and substance of it, is only sharp and poysonous pricks".[7]

Kirke was wilfully blind; but he was right when he stated that the agricultural community disliked the idea of trees near their fields. To show how strong was this antagonism it is only necessary to give two examples from Urie in Kincardineshire.[75] The first was in 1682: "The Laird and blazie ordained the heall tennentis of both baronies to set and plant trees yeirlie in their respective yeardes, to wit, ashes, plains, birkes, fir or rountrie, geintrie. To wit everie husbandmane yeirlie sex trees, everie cottar three, and everie grasman two trees yeirlie." The fines were then stated, ranging from "eight poundis" to "twentie shilling", if the tenant did not go to the gardener to receive his trees at Michaelmas or March.

The second example dates from 1733, and is particularly interesting in showing that even after a lapse of fifty-one years the tenants still made both passive and active resistance against planting. It states that even after many laudable laws and acts had been passed to enforce planting, "the whole Barrony of Urie is now inteirly destitute of planting" . . . "and hereby ordains the present gairdner of Urie to plant trees in the respective yeards of the whole Barrony. And in regard some trees formerly planted have been inteirly spoylled in the grouth, not only by cutting and breaking thereof, but likewise by digging and cutting the roots of the trees so planted with their spades." It was therefore ordained that "all within the said Barrony shall hereafter leave unlaboured a strip of ground round their respective yeard dykes, not under two feet and ane half of measure for preserving the said trees". Fines up to twenty pounds (Scots) were to be given for defacement or damage of any kind, and to make this even more drastic the tenant was held responsible for the trees on his land.

In pre-Restoration times trees mentioned by name are usually Sycamores. They were growing at Gala House and at Seton Castle long before the Commonwealth and must have been fairly common. That curious Cromwellian trooper, Richard Frank, who was so much more interested in fishing than soldiering, wrote about "the flourishing fields of Mighill beautified and adorned with stately Sycomores".

For long the opinion was held that many trees

were not hardy in Scotland, but others commonly planted were Alder, Elder, Ash, Birch, Beech, Elm and Scots Pine. Although Oaks at one time formed an almost virgin forest along the foothills of the Grampians, their name is rarely met with during the seventeenth century. Exotic trees were seldom planted until later. Loudon quotes Dr. Walker [44] when he gives the date of introduction to Scotland of a few of them, among them the Lime, planted at Taymouth in 1664, the Laburnum at Panmure in Angus in 1696 and the Carolina Bird Cherry at Hopetoun in 1743.

Both Defoe and Macky expressed surprise and admiration at the numbers of trees to be seen growing on large lowland estates. Although both travellers made their tours about 1720, it is obvious that a great many, both hardwoods and conifers, had been planted shortly after the Restoration. Defoe wrote: "You hardly see a gentleman's house, as you pass the Louthains, towards Edinburgh, but they are distinguish'd by groves and walks of Firr-trees about them".[21] Oddly enough he complained about their quality, and explained that they were often kept in the nurseries until they were 12 or 15 feet high when they were planted out unstaked. He gave this as a definite reason for poor condition: "The tree is bended every way, the earth loosen'd continually about it, the root is often stirr'd, and the tree gets no time to strike root into the earth".[21]

Mass planting in parks and estates, as opposed to shelter trees close to houses, did not commence until after 1660. Then a few enthusiasts began at once on a

47

large scale. Both travellers were full of praise of
Yester in Midlothian. Defoe wrote that the old Earl
of Tweeddale, a favourite of Charles II, and his successor planted 6000 acres from 1664 onwards. Macky
recounts how "The palace of Yester stands in the
middle of the best planted park I ever saw: the park
walls are about eight miles in circumference; and I
dare venture to say, there is a million of full grown
trees in it. In short, it's larger, as well walled, and
more regularly planted than Richmond in Surrey."[49]
He thought that the woods at Dupplin were fully
better, although they were not quite so old as those
at Yester.

These accounts show that large plantations were
made at Yester before those at Tyninghame, where
the Earl of Haddington is usually quoted as having
made the first plantations in Scotland. Actually
massed planting at Tyninghame did not commence
until about 1702. Macky wrote that the Earl of
Haddington "hath planted many millions of trees in
a sandy down or links and they thrive mightily. He
hath also laid out several avenues through his park,
which, when full grown, will be as noble as any in
Britain."[49] Neither author mentions the famous
Holly hedges which were planted about 1705 and
comprised 2952 yards in 1835. One walk, 743 yards
long, had hedges on either side 11 feet in breadth and
and 15 feet high; another hedge, planted as a protection on the east side of the garden, reached 25 feet in
height.[66]

Avenues were also being made to big houses, sometimes of trees planted as specimens, sometimes of

FIG. VI.—HATTON HOUSE, AT ONE TIME THE GREATEST FORMAL GARDEN IN SCOTLAND

FROM A PRINT OF ABOUT 1710

rides cut through plantations. Defoe and Macky mention them frequently. In Angus both Glamis and Panmure are praised. At Glamis "the great avenue is a full half mile, planted on either side with several rows of trees", while at Panmure the avenue was "cut through a wood half a mile in length bordered by a fine high hedge". Others specially noted were those at Traquair, Broxmouth and Alloa where there were "woods with vistas cut through 150 acres".

It will be seen that sufficient planting was being carried out on large estates by the end of the seventeenth century to act as focal points for the more general spread of woods which began as soon as times improved. One gets a fair idea of how trees were generally used at this period from an examination of Slezer's *Theatrum Scotica* of 1693, the first pictorial work to be published on Scotland. A number of the plates are of ruined Abbeys and are of little interest to us, but most of the remaining plates depict bird's-eye views of towns. In these the trees are invariably shown planted in rows for shelter, are almost always only half grown and are always hardwoods. In later editions there are a few additional plates of great houses and gardens, probably drawn at the beginning of the eighteenth century, of which three are reproduced in this volume. In these the same style of planting is seen: only in one is there a row of Conifers, in the foreground of the garden of Hatton, which is miscalled Argile House on the original plate. The drawings were done by an unknown artist, probably a Dutchman, but it is known

49   E

that he visited each subject, and there is no reason to believe that they are not faithful representations of what he saw.

Stress has been laid on the growth of planting, as it was essential in the process of evolution of the garden in Scotland.

2

The Formal Garden

Pleasure gardens of this period differed little from those in England. It was an age of formality which towards the middle of the eighteenth century reached such a pitch that the pendulum swung to the other extreme and the landscape gardener with his ideas, often carried to absurd lengths, of improving on Nature became the fashion. Our gardens did not follow quite such a stilted pattern of formality; but those who designed them deliberately set out to imitate English gardens, which in turn followed the French, Italian and Dutch styles.

It is known that several of the best English garden designers of the day, such as London and Wise, and Switzer, drew up plans for, and superintended the making of, some Scottish gardens. Among the largest was Hatton, a seat of the Earl of Lauderdale, which was designed by London and Wise, who also supplied a foreman to superintend the work. Plans, sections and sample sacks of earth were sent from Hatton to London. Loudon, who is usually quoted as the authority for these statements, unfortunately gives few details; indeed, he is deliberately vague. It is singularly difficult to find direct evidence of the actual identity of the designers of our large gardens. Possibly too much stress has been laid on the direct influence of these English garden architects; and also on the supposition that great gardens were designed and completed as one unit. Scottish gardeners even at this period were in charge of many of the greatest English gardens and were quite capable not only of acting as head gardeners but also of laying out and making gardens. It is likely that a few of them were repatriated to design and take charge of some of our gardens.

None of our own people stand out as great garden designers. Sir William Bruce, the architect of Holyrood in the reign of Charles II, was able to ornament a garden, as is seen from the charming stone-work in his own garden at Kinross House, but whether he went further and designed parterres and the general lay-out of flower-beds and borders is not known. His pupil, William Adam, the father of the famous brothers, certainly designed some gardens in the formal style of London and Wise, among them a proposed lay-out for Arniston in 1726.[57] These designs, however, were only by-products of his architecture, and none were sufficiently striking to be labelled as Adam gardens by future generations. Many of the houses, of which he is known to have been the architect, had no formal gardens attached.

The truth is that these formal gardens were so stereotyped in design that they were easily copied. Most of the books of the day dealing with garden making were fully illustrated, and any gardener or

51

clerk of the works who was intelligent could adapt some existing plan to any ordinary site.

Even John Reid, whose book *The Scots Gard'ner* was the first devoted to gardening to be published in Scotland,[61] made no attempt to break away from the normal in his suggestions for pleasure gardens. It is only when he deals with the kitchen garden that we notice fresh ideas creeping in.

John Reid is a puzzling figure in our horticulture. He wrote this one book and disappeared from ken. He mentioned that he was born near Niddrie Castle, seven miles west of Edinburgh, and in the preface to the third edition it is stated that he was gardener to Sir George Mackenzie, Bart., of Rosehaugh on the Moray Firth, the famous "Bloody" Mackenzie, Advocate to Charles II. Even Reid's name is forgotten in the neighbourhood of Fort Rose; yet he must have had a garden training extremely advanced for his day. His book is full of sound information on preparing the site for a garden, levelling, making paths and walls, planting, and particularly on tilling the ground and the cultivation of flowers, fruit and vegetables.

The book starts with an imaginative plan of a house surrounded by a square of inner gardens divided by paths so that each garden formed an equilateral triangle. These inner gardens were in turn surrounded by a wide expanse of orchards and woodland, the whole being octagonal in shape. Reid drew particular attention to the importance of the house being in the centre of the garden. "Make all the buildings and plantings ly so about the house, as that the house may be the centre; all the walks, trees,

and hedges running to the house. Therefore, whatever you have on the one hand, make as much, of the
same forme and in the same place, on the other."[61]
From what is known of gardens of the period, it is
unlikely that his exact plans were actually followed
in any particular instance.

His instructions on pleasure gardens were much in
keeping with the general practice of the time.
"Pleasure-gardens useth to be divided into walks and
plots, with a bordure round each plot; and at the
corner of each, may be a holly, or some such shrub,
train'd up, some pyramidal, others spherical; the
trees and shrubs at the wall plyed and prun'd, the
greens thereon cut in several figures, the walkes
layed with gravel, and the plots within the grass (in
several places whereof may be flower-pots), the
bordures boxed, and planted with variety of fine
flowers orderly intermixt, weeded, mow'd, rolled,
and kept all clean and handsome."

Outer courts had to "have only one bordure at the
wall, planted with laurels and other greens; one
pathed or brick-walle in the middle, leading to the
middle of the front-house, with a long grass-plot on
each hand".

His ideas on borders in the kitchen garden are
particularly interesting, as here we see an early sign
of the mixture of vegetables, fruit and flowers which
are such a delightful feature of so many Scottish
gardens to-day. Reid wrote: "The bordures of your
kitchen-garden, round by the walkes, may be boxed
with thyme, lavender, hysop, rue, &c., the next with
parsley, straw-berries, violets, July-flowers, &c.,

53

cherrie-gardens and physick-gardens, with sweet-brier often cut, or box cut three times per annum, in April, June and August, remembering to cut their roots inside every second year, that they exhaust not the strength or nourishment of the flowers or herbs. But that which I preferre for flower-gardens above all is dwarf-juniper, raised from seed and planted."

The conventions attached to seventeenth and early eighteenth century gardening in Scotland continued in many cases to be used through several generations. Although excessive formalities, such as parterres and topiary work, may have disappeared, yet the general lay-out remained, or was added to from time to time, and fitted in well with the elaborate bedding systems of the early and mid-Victorian eras. Thus, where these great gardens still existed in the nineteenth century, it is often difficult to separate the original conception from additions made in after years. Drumlanrig and Drummond Castle are examples of formal gardens which have existed over two centuries. It is quite impossible to say how much of the original design remains.

In a few instances contemporary plans or illustrations still exist, such as those of Arniston and Dalkeith, Hatton and Culross. The plans of Arniston are interesting as showing three distinct styles. First is a plan of the policies prior to 1690 with the old U-shaped house in the middle of an enclosure about a hundred yards square, simple and even crude in its ideas. The second is a plan of a proposed lay-out in 1726, extremely elaborate with great parterres on two sides of the house, a kitchen garden and orchard

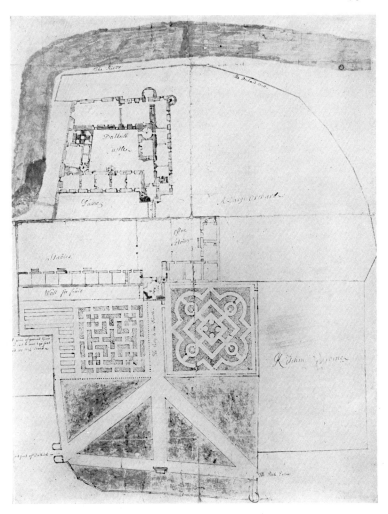

FIG. VII.—A PLAN FOR THE FORMAL GARDEN AT DALKEITH,
PROBABLY DESIGNED ABOUT 1690

on a third and a straight avenue bordered with trees sweeping up to the front of the house. This is the plan that was probably supplied by William Adam. It was never completed, but part must have been carried out, for Chief Baron Dundas described how his great-grandfather, the First President of the Court of Session, "at very great expense formed the cascade in the gardeners' park, which was let off when he and his guests sat down at dinner, and continued to run for about an hour. The aqueduct which filled the reservoir pond at the top of the bank was brought off by a dam immediately beneath the junction of the Deanhead and Castleton burns. I just recollect, and that is all, the taking down of the cascade, some time I think about 1764, when the present garden was made by my father."[67]

The third plan shows the gardens and policies as they were finally carried out by the second President Dundas; the plan was made about 1753. It is much simpler with a single parterre on one side of the house, but the policies were elaborately treated under the influence of the landscape school of garden design.

The plan of the garden at Dalkeith, a seat of the Duke of Buccleuch, is reproduced in Fig. VII. The exact date is unknown but must be somewhere about 1700 as the garden was in the course of making in 1702. The house occupies a corner made by a bend in the river. The view from the front of the house was picturesque, looking down over the steep banks, yet the lay-out was unfortunate in having the stables between the house and gardens, but this could hardly be avoided. Two avenues converged and led between two parterres before going under a three-storied gate-house leading to a small court and the main entrance. These parterres show two representative variants, both of which were common at that period in England and Scotland, one a conventional design of rectangles, the other a more elaborate scroll pattern. Dalkeith was frequently enlarged and improved during the eighteenth century. Considerable alterations were in progress at the time of Defoe's visit about 1720, as he mentioned water-works, fountains and a canal designed but not completed, as well as fine avenues in course of planting. The height of its importance as a ducal residence was at the end of the century and early in the nineteenth when additions and improvements were carried out in the grand manner. Even Robert Adam was called in to design "a Doric Bridge of 70 feet span over which it is intended to pass in the new approach from Edinburgh to Dalkeith House" (see Fig. XII).

The garden at Drumlanrig, also belonging to the Duke of Buccleuch, was started about 1720, and was planned on an even more elaborate scale. This was the garden that inspired Defoe, who hated hills, to his famous description, "like a fine picture in a dirty grotto, or like an equestrian statue set up in a barn". The garden obviously impressed him, although he was a trifle vague in his description: "At the extent of the gardens there are pavillions and banqueting-houses, exactly answering to one another, and the greens trimm'd, spaliers and hedges are in perfection".

We have a further account by the Rev. Peter Rae (1700–1740) in which he wrote: "The gardens of Drumlanrig are very beautiful. The regular gardens, with one to be made on the back of the plumbery, the outer court before the house, and the house itself, make nine square plots of ground, whereof the kitchen garden, the court before the house, and the garden designed make three; my lady Duchess's garden, the house, and the last parterre and the flower garden make other three, that is nine in all, and the castle is in the centre. As to those called irregular gardens, because the course of the Parkburn would not allow them to be square, they are very pretty and well suited to one another. They call one part thereof Virginia, the other Barbados (from their peculiar shapes); there goes a large gravel walk down betwixt them from the south parterre to the cascade."[60] Apart from the cascade which has been removed, the gardens at Drumlanrig existed up to a few years ago in much the same form as in the eighteenth century, with the hanging gardens cut out of the rock which were admired by Macky and Defoe.[19]

Contemporary descriptions of such gardens as Yester, Pinkie, Leslie, Hopetoun and the Earl of Moray's garden at Holyrood mention the parterres, *jets d'eau*, evergreens and vistas in terms very similar to those of large gardens in the south. Macky wrote of Yester that "The parterre and garden behind the house is very spacious and fine. There is a handsome basin with a jett d'eaux in the middle of the parterre, with four good statues upon pedestals at each corner.

There is abundance of evergreens, and green slopes, regularly dispos'd; and to the west of the garden on an artificial mound is a pleasant summerhouse."

Leslie was noted in the early eighteenth century for its full-grown trees and magnificent garden. "There's a noble parterre to the east, cut out into green slopes, adorn'd with evergreens, and from the parterre on the south of the house is a long terras walk, and under it five several terrasses, to which you descend by stately stairs to another square garden by the riverside with a water-work in the middle."

While the garden at Hatton, designed by London and Wise, was probably the most formal in Scotland (see Fig. VI), the gardens of Culross, near where Fife joins Clackmannan, were among the largest, so large, indeed, that the Earl of Mar was heard to remark that he thanked God they were not his, for the expense of keeping up the gardens would ruin him. They are seen in Fig. VIII. The treatment of the park land between the kitchen and formal gardens is interesting with its planting in rows and straight vistas, a practice that was anathema to the landscape gardeners of the next generation. You will notice the number of walls; each garden, and even the two orchards, have their individual walls. Hedges were far from common; in fact, one of the few examples of garden hedges in contemporary plans and illustrations of this period is that enclosing the main garden of the College of Glasgow (Fig. X).

In one particular some of these great Scottish gardens differed from those in the south, the almost excessive use of statuary. Of Glamis Defoe wrote:

58

FIG. VIII.—THE HOUSE AND GARDENS OF CULROSS ABOUT 1700

"When you come to the outer gate you are surpris'd with the variety and beauty of the statues, busts, some of stone, some of brass, some gilded, some plain. The statues in brass are four, one of King James VI, one of King Charles I booted and spurr'd, as if going to take horse at the head of his army; one of Charles II habited à la Hero, which the world knows he had nothing of about him; one of King James VII after the pattern of that at Whitehall." Macky describes the parterre at Broxmouth as adorned with statues behind it. At Newbattle, "in the area between the avenue and the outer gate, is the statue of a gladiator; and on each side of the gate there is a stone pavilion; and through four square green courts you come to the palace, each of the first three courts having rows of statues on each side, as big as the life; and in the fourth court the biggest holley trees I ever saw". Hopetoun also had its statues: "The parterre fronting the Salloon hath a large bason of water at bottom: it's also adorn'd with a multitude of statues on pedestals. From the terras to the north of this parterre is the finest view I ever saw anywhere."

So far we have dealt with large gardens. If we look back at the history of such smaller gardens as belong to this period, we find that they were often owned by a branch of one of the great families or by some servant of the Crown with a satisfactory income. The average laird could not spare the land for policies or anything so unproductive of income as a pleasure garden until agriculture began to give him a better return or commerce flowed again in Scotland. Everything that could be made to bear rent, whether in money or kind, was kept under the plough. In some old houses it is still possible to see signs of tilled fields close under the front windows. A narrow strip of grass separated the house from tillage or pasture, and the garden abutted on one of the sides of the house, making a very compact domain, usually sheltered from the prevailing wind by a narrow belt of hardwoods. Such a fashion was more in keeping with the times, homely and very pleasant if the garden were well tended. Kellie Castle in Fife was an excellent example. The late Sir Robert Lorimer much approved of this fashion. Of Kellie Castle he wrote: "I always think the ideal plan is to have the park, with the sheep or beasts grazing in it, coming right under the windows at one side, and the gardens attached to the house at another side".[51]

These small gardens were almost all of simple design. That of Stobhall, still in existence on the high banks of the Tay almost opposite Stanley, is rectangular. Looking from the front windows it requires little imagination to picture it as it was with straight walks dividing the little garden into square beds and old pyramidal Yews or clipped Box standing sentinel at their corners. In the beds would be Hollyhocks and Sunflowers, Coxcombs and Bella Donnas, a very peaceful scene with the purr of the Tay below to soothe the ears. It is a pity that so few of these gardens still exist, for they are much more typical of an old Scottish garden than the great expanse of Hatton or Drummond Castle.

Most gardens of this period followed the forms already described: a few were exceptional, either from the composition of the site or owing to some eccentricity of the owner. Terraced, or hanging, gardens were not uncommon where the terrain allowed their construction; in fact, John Reid instructed his readers how to make retaining walls for terraces.

Certainly the most famous garden of this kind was Barncluith on the outskirts of Hamilton. Its Dutch garden, of earlier date, was mentioned in the previous chapter. The terraces, however, were certainly made after the Restoration. These are cut out of the steep bank of a gorge on the river Avon. The declivity is very steep, with the result that the retaining walls are proportionately high and the terraces narrow. They have been so altered and extended that it is quite impossible to unravel the threads and say what belongs to the late seventeenth and what to the early eighteenth centuries; but they must have been more or less completed about 1725 when Macky described Barncluith as "a very romantick garden, called Baron cleuh, which consists of seven hanging terras-walks, down to a river side. In some of those walks are banquetting-houses, with walks and grottos, and all of them fill'd with large evergreens, in the shapes of beasts and birds."

Barncluith was one of the gardens most often described by bygone writers. The personal criticisms that usually accompanied these descriptions are interesting as showing the trend of garden thought at the time when they were written: for instance, Sir Walter Scott was mildly enthusiastic: "It might be thought that the house and garden of Barncluith,

with its walks of velvet turf and its verdant alleys of
yew and holly, would seem incongruous among natural
scenes as magnificent as those we have described. But
the effect produced is exactly the contrary. The place
is so small, that its decorations, while they form, from
their antique appearance, a singular foreground, cannot compete with, far less subdue the solemn grandeur
of the view which you look down upon; and thus give
the spectator the idea of a hermitage in the midst of
the wilderness." Later, Gorrie, who was one of the
foremost Scottish gardening writers of mid-Victorian
days, was much offended by its picturesque formality,
if such an expression can be used. In describing
Barncluith he wrote: "The era of geometrical gardening comes in an age when taste is half educated, but
not so much cultivated as to prevent it from taking itself up with puerilities, frivolities and monstrosities".

Another garden of somewhat similar character,
only a few miles away, is Dalzell. There certainly was
an old garden which may have consisted of one or
more terraces, but the famous terrace, which with its
box-edged portion is to-day quoted as a perfect
example of an old Scottish formal garden, was only
made in the middle of the last century. It was designed
by the late Lord Hamilton of Dalzell along with that
excellent architect, R. W. Billings, who lived for
several years at Dalzell. It is difficult to imagine a
more charmingly gardened terrace, or one which has
not only the appearance but also the spirit of the age.
It is also an object-lesson to the gardening historian,
for it should teach him that appearances of age are
deceptive.

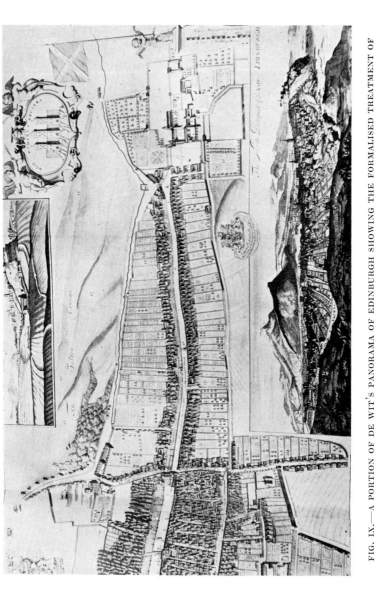

FIG. IX.—A PORTION OF DE WIT'S PANORAMA OF EDINBURGH SHOWING THE FORMALISED TREATMENT OF TOWN GARDENS AT THE BEGINNING OF THE EIGHTEENTH CENTURY

The garden of Preston, near Edinburgh, was most peculiar, as the owner, Lord Grange, must have modelled it on his conception of an Elizabethan garden. "During the Rebellion (1715), and some time after, Lord Grange amused himself in laying out and planting a fine garden, full of close walks and labyrinths and wildernesses, which, though it did not occupy above four or five acres, cost one at least two hours to perambulate. This garden or pleasure-ground was soon brought to perfection by his defending it from the westerly and south-westerly winds by hedges of common elder, which in a few years were above sixteen feet high, and completely sheltered all the interior grounds. This garden continued to be an object of curiosity down to the year 1740, insomuch that flocks of company resorted to it from Edinburgh, during the summer, on Saturdays and Mondays, for Sunday was not at that time a day of pleasure, and were highly gratified by the sight, there being nothing like it in Scotland, except at Alloa, the seat of the Earl of Mar, of which indeed it was a copy in miniature."[12] The Preston garden was so compact that it can have borne little resemblance to Alloa with its great gardens which at that time exceeded 40 acres in extent, including a terrace of large proportions.

So many of the large formal gardens were in the neighbourhood of Edinburgh that the city dwellers were vastly impressed. De Wit's panorama of the city from the south shows clearly how the gardens of all houses of any size were laid out in miniature parterres. The scale of the panorama is so small and the numbers of gardens so large that it was impossible that all of them should have followed so stereotyped a plan; but De Wit, living as he did in Edinburgh, must have had some grounds for their inclusion.

One of the larger gardens on the outskirts belonged to the Palace of the Earl of Moray at Holyrood. Behind the house was a large parterre with four terraces, at the bottom of which was a bowling-green with a handsome pavilion at one end.

A public garden in Edinburgh was projected as early as 1662. This is one of those curious anomalies which are occasionally found in the domestic annals of our country, for this was during a period when our cities had scarcely outgrown their ultra-conservative spirit. John Thomson, a gardener, was ordered to prepare a plan for a garden in Parliament Close, which was to be layed out in walks and to be planted with trees, herbs and flowers, as well as Cabbages and "other common garden stuff". The plan showed the western end planted with Plum and Cherry trees bordered with Gooseberries, Currants and Roses, and flowers set along the south wall.[44] Unfortunately this garden was never made.

Further to the north the fertile land bordering the Moray Firth was rapidly being improved both in agriculture and in gardening, possibly from the presence in that district of John Reid, but chiefly from the example of Elizabeth Mordaunt, daughter of the Earl of Peterborough, who married the eldest son of the Duke of Gordon in 1706 and came to live in Scotland. Two proprietors at once set about improving their estates, Sir Robert Gordon of Gordonston and Sir William Gordon of Invergordon, and soon they were among the best in the north. But further afield conditions altered little. Sir Archibald Grant (the second baronet) has left an account of Monymusk as he found it in 1716.

"By the indulgence of a very worthy father I was allowed, though then very young, to begin to enclose and plant, and provide and prepare nurseries. At that time there was not one acre upon the whole estate enclosed, nor any timber upon it but a few elm, sycamore and ash, about a small kitchen-garden adjoining to the house, and some straggling trees at some of the farmyards, with a small copse-wood, not enclosed and dwarfish, and browsed by sheep and cattle. All the farms were ill-disposed and mixed, different persons having alternate ridges; not one wheel-carriage on the estate, nor indeed any one road that would allow it. The house was an old castle, with battlements and six different roofs of various heights and directions, confusedly and inconveniently combined, and all rotten, with two wings more modern of two stories only, the half of the windows of the higher rising above the roofs; with granaries, stables, and houses for all cattle and the vermin attending them close adjoining; and with the heath and muir reaching in angles or gushets to the gate, and much heath near. What land was in culture belonged to the farms, by which their cattle and dung were always at the door. The whole land was raised and uneven, and full of stones, many of them very large, and all the ridges crooked in shape of an S, and very high, and full of noxious weeds, and poor, being worn out by culture, without proper manure or

F

tillage. Much of the land near the house was poor and boggy. The people were poor, ignorant, and slothful, and ingrained enemies to planting, enclosing, or any improvements or cleanness; no keeping of sheep or cattle, or roads, but four months, when oats and bere was on the ground. The farm-houses, and even corn-mills, and manse and school were all poor, dirty huts, occasionly pulled in pieces for manure, or which fell of themselves almost each alternate year." [72]

That does not give us a pretty picture of what afterwards became one of the finest estates in that part of Scotland. If the highland laird could put up with that kind of life, he had no use for gardening. If he could not, and could afford it, he lived elsewhere. So we are forced to the conclusion that, with a few exceptions and round the fertile coastal districts, gardening languished in the highlands until a much later date.

3

Garden Practice

During this period the knowledge of the technique of gardening in its several branches was almost entirely confined to professional gardeners. One occasionally hears of owners who took an interest in their gardens, but very rarely did they show any aptitude for horticulture or for any technical operations. The fact that exact knowledge was confined to a professional class certainly contributed to the slow spread of gardening among the middle and lower classes. Apart from lacking the requisite knowledge they must have had few opportunities of acquiring any but the commonest plants. While nurserymen and seedsmen are known to have traded in Edinburgh shortly after the Restoration, general communications were so bad until near the middle of the eighteenth century, that delivery of plants and seeds at a distance was slow and uncertain, unless the garden owner visited the capital or had an agent or friends living there.

Thus we have to rely on large gardens for instances of, and professional gardeners for information on, garden practice. Because in the eighteenth century this lagged little behind England in most branches of gardening proves that the Scottish gardener was a skilled workman. In many cases he had to contend with a very conservative owner and the innate supposition that a vast number of plants would not grow in our climate. In addition, as planting increased, he usually found himself with a great deal of extra work on his hands, as it was customary for plantations to be under the charge of the gardener, a practice that survived until the nineteenth century was well advanced.

One of the sources for information on garden technique is *The Scots Gard'ner*. One would suspect that John Reid had been trained in an English garden if it were not for the fact that he showed no practical experience of tender plants, which were coming into fashion in England at the date of his book, and that he could not divorce himself from the universal Scottish practice of run-rigging his ground.

For centuries this had been the curse of our

agriculture, and in due course its use crept into gardens. Its origin was curiously communal, a subdivision of the fields among the inhabitants of the farm towns. The fields were subdivided into long and narrow strips so that any particularly productive land should not fall into the hands of one tenant. This division was done by forming ridges 10 or 12 feet across with shallow gulleys between the ridges. The earth taken from the gulleys was used for heightening the ridge. Run-rigging persisted in out-of-the-way parts of the country until the nineteenth century. In some fields long in permanent pasture the remains of the ridges are still to be seen. Such a method did not allow proper cultivation; it was extremely wasteful of land, as the shallow gulleys were left fallow so that there should be no suspicion of encroachment, and heavy rain washed seed from the ridges into the gulleys where it was wasted.

Reid advocated this system for the kitchen garden, one of the few mistakes in garden technique to be found in his book. He wrote: "Keep the ground well open and void for kitchen-herbs and roots; which must be orderly divided into ridges". There is no doubt he meant run-rigging, as he described the usual garden furrow later in the same chapter.

He was a firm believer in thorough digging: "At the autumnal fallowing, delve or plow deep, and apply hot unrotted and uncompounded manures; at spring re-plow or re-delve, and apply such manures as have layn mixed and rotted with earth; then mix, rake or harrow". Most authorities are inclined to blame the Scots for not improving their land. If

FIG. X.—THE COLLEGE OF GLASGOW AND ITS GARDENS AT THE END OF THE
SEVENTEENTH CENTURY

Reid's advice was followed, that was certainly not the case in gardens, for what he wrote on manuring is very complete. He described how he made a pit in which all kinds of manures were collected and allowed to "lye a year at least, but not above two. Then I take them out, and then stirre, air, mingle and work them with fresh earth or by themselves, as I have occasion, till they become sweet and of an agreeable scent, yet retaining their virtue; this frees them from the noxious qualities they other wayes retaine, and consequently are not so apt to gender or produce worms, weeds, and mushrooms, instead of wholesome and pleasant plants, fruits, and roots for the table. Observe what manures are proper for the soil. All hot manures are proper for cold, stiff, and moist grounds. So all rotten and cold manures are proper for dry and hot grounds. All manures that retain moisture, are for poor, sandy, and gravelly soils." He then went on to describe each kind in detail.

He advised the use of water that had been brought to the temperature of the air in tubs, the application of liquid manure, the advantages of watering flower-pots from below, and the constant working of the hoe in dry weather. He warned his readers against watering young foliage in spring while there was a danger of cold nights. In fact, one cannot read a page of his book without being impressed by his common sense.

What he and other gardeners of his time lacked was a knowledge of draining. At the end of the eighteenth and beginning of the nineteenth century one comes across a number of cases of kitchen gardens which had either to be shifted bodily to a new site or to have thousands of cartloads of old sour soil removed and fresh loam laid to a depth of several feet in its place after the ground had been drained.

Scotland was not far behind in the cultivation and propagation of fruit, which was now becoming more plentiful even on estates where general gardening was neglected. There are frequent entries in old account books of the purchase of fruit trees and grafts.

"ffor the Laird of Gordonetoun

MUREHOUSE, ffebruarie 18, 1684.

SIR,—In complyance to yours, I have caused deliver to your servant, a dozen or foureteen grafts of the Great-Red-Straik aple, foure of the Great-French-Rubie aple, some of the Gray Pepin, some of the Great-Summer-Bon-Chrestien peare, some of the Great-French-Bergamot peare, some of the Longueville peare, and severall other of the best peares and aples I have, whose names I cannot tell, my gardner not being at home, but they are al excellent fruits. Those that I know, are bound up together with their naimes, and carefully wrapt up in ane hay rope, which I heartily wish may hold, and have good successe with you, as they do here; so I remayne, Sir, your humble servant,

"MR J. HUNTER" [24]

Before 1700 Apples were grafted on Paradise stock, Pears on Quince and sweet Cherries on Morello stocks. From the number of entries for Pear and Apple seed one can judge that many gardeners must have raised their own varieties, and probably trees on their own roots, which may account for the many exceptionally poor kinds that were so often found in old Scottish gardens. Bush fruit was increased by suckers or cuttings and Strawberries by runners. The cultivation of small fruit differed very little from the present methods.

Pruning tree fruit was rough and ready, but served the purpose when carried out by the rule-of-thumb but unscientific method that persisted in many gardens until the twentieth century. John Reid bluntly scolded those who neglected to prune their fruit trees, particularly during the first few years: "Yea, the first five or six years, and then they fall a-massackering, at which time the branches being growen, some of them greater than others, now run away with all the nourishment from the smaller, insomuch that no man can reduce them to order again".

Glasshouses were unknown before the end of the century, although Reid wrote that several tried to grow "Indian and Spanish-jasmines, mirtles, oleanders and orange-trees". His instructions, however, are so vague that it is doubtful if he spoke from actual knowledge. On the other hand, hot-beds were common in all the larger gardens. Reid gives accurate instructions, while glass for hot-beds is a frequent item in account-books, such as the *Household Book* of Lady Grizel Baillie.[2] Among the MS. accounts at Dalkeith is one dated 1702, "Account for Glaswork to James Waugh, 3 windows in hotbeds 87 feets at 5 shillings a feet".[20] Bell glasses were also in use.

In the flower garden herbaceous plants were increased by slips, offsets, layers and seed. Most seed was sown in October and the pots placed in a frame with a glass light against a south wall until the spring. Primroses and Cowslips were divided in spring or after they flowered in July. Roses were almost always pruned in October. Offsets of bulbs were removed from the parent bulb in June or July, stored in a dry place and planted out in September or October.

It will be seen that, with the exception of greenhouses and forcing, garden practice did not differ greatly except in detail from what we are accustomed to to-day.

A garden account for 1702 [20] gives the prices for "Workloomes for the gardine":

four speeds	at lib 2–0–6 (Scots)
two reacks	at 18 pens per piece
two gardine hous	at 10 pens per piece
ane scyeth	lib 1–10–0

This seems to have been the average price for the time.

Gardeners appear to have been very badly paid, particularly when it is taken into consideration that they also had to look after the tree nurseries and superintend the plantations. In 1723 the gardener at Gordonston in Moray, a much improved estate, received a free house but probably had to supply his own food out of his wages which came to £12:10s. sterling a year.[24] The gardener at Cawdor was paid mostly in kind and received 12 bolls of meal a year in 1718. Garden labourers were usually paid at the rate of 5d. sterling a day during the first half of the eighteenth century, but this was only paid for services rendered; in bad weather or during the off-seasons they were unpaid. Weeding was usually done by women, a practice that continued in many gardens until Victorian days.

4

Plants

TREES AND SHRUBS. — Prior to the eighteenth century great difficulty is experienced in giving the modern equivalent for the names of garden flowers. In any case the flora of the usual Scottish garden was very small until after 1700. The famous botanist, John Ray, was one of the first men to examine our native flora during a journey through the country in 1661. From the very occasional references he gave to gardens, one can judge that he was not impressed; but he does mention a garden near Linlithgow: "This Mr Stuart, one of the bailiffs of the town, hath nourished in his garden various exotick plants, more than one could hope for in so northerly and cold a country; some such as we had not before seen, viz. Archangelica, Fumaria siliquosa, Carduus lacteus peregrinus flo. albo, Verbascum 4 Matth, angustifolium, Anchusa species flo. parvo nigricante, Alcea surrecta laevis flo. amplo rubro et albo, as we then named them". Only three have been traced with any certainty; Archangelica is *Archangelica officinalis*, Fumaria siliquosa is *Corydalis bulbosa* and Verbascum 4 Matth. angustifolium is *Phlomis Lychnitis*.

The strictly formal garden was not a good medium for growing a great variety of plants. The more intricate the design in which the parterre was fashioned the more limited was the selection of plants that could be grown, for they had to conform to very definite limits of size. Still it was remarkable what a variety was in fairly common cultivation.

Hedges consisted almost entirely of Thorn or Holly: it is odd that Yew hedges at this period were not very common in Scotland, although Yews of columnar habit were often planted as standards in the corners of beds or at the end of terraces.

Flowering shrubs were rarely grown, as they did not fit into the scheme of the severely formal garden. Such as were planted were Lilacs, *Daphne Mezereon* and, more rarely, *Arbutus Unedo*, with Jasmine, *Clematis Vitalba* and Honeysuckle on walls, while Pyracantha is occasionally mentioned. Even Roses did not appear to be particularly popular until later, and consisted mostly of the Musk and the old Double Yellow. The only popular flowering tree was the Gean, *Prunus Avium*. This was always a popular tree in Scotland and was frequently planted as a specimen near houses. The accompanying illustration (photographed in 1880) (Fig. XI) shows an old tree growing at Glendoick in eastern Perthshire. From its size it must have been of great age, probably dating from the house, about 1736. Laburnums also increased in popularity; a little later they were often planted in walks through policies and in shrubberies. The remains of a Laburnum walk still exists at Camperdown. From the size of some of the original butts, over 2 feet in diameter, they must be very old, possibly seedlings from Panmure, not far away,

74

FIG. XI.—AN OLD GEAN AT GLENDOICK. FROM A PHOTOGRAPH
TAKEN ABOUT 1880

where it was first introduced in 1696.

Woody plants in great demand were evergreens that grew into shapely and compact specimens, or could easily be trained or cut into shape, such as *Arbor Vitae*, Privet, Box, *Juniperus Sabina* and a Conifer that went under the general name of Cypress. Topiary work, which was so popular in gardens of this period, was usually carved out of Yew, Holly, *Phyllyrea angustifolia* and, occasionally, *Rhamnus Alaternus*.

An immense amount of labour must have been spent each year in some gardens in keeping these evergreens in shape. In almost all old accounts one comes across entries for the snedding, or pruning, knife. Most large establishments grew these evergreens from seed in their own nurseries, partly for convenience and partly owing to the poor quality of purchased plants. Occasionally there are references to nurserymen, such as the biting complaint of Lady Grizel Baillie about young trees "bought of John Hope which was a perfit cheat."

FLOWERS.—Probably the most popular of all flowers in Scotland at this time was the Clove Pink, which was mentioned more often than any other flower grown purely for beauty and scent. They were usually grown from seed, but good varieties were recognized, and were increased by the common method of slips. Not only were they grown in beds but also in pots; Reid advised his readers "to preserve the choicest from too much raines, by laying the pots on their sides; strick off the snow when it lyes too weightie on them".

Other favourites were Stocks, Bears-ears (Auriculas), Anemones, Ranunculus, Hollyhocks, Jonquils, Sweet Williams, Tulips and Cockscomb (*Celosia cristata*). In larger gardens there was greater variety, and some of the plants mentioned are surprising, such as *Anemone triloba*, *Gentiana acaulis*, Columbines, Cyclamens, *Tradescantia virginica*, Crocus, Colchicum, Ornithogalum, Peonies, Aconite and Hellebore.

Among biennials and annuals the choice was not so great. Those most commonly grown were Love-lies-bleeding (*Amaranthus caudatus*), Marvel of Peru (*Mirabilis Jalapa*), African Marigold, Convolvulus, double Marigolds, Nigella, annual Delphiniums, Antirrhinums, double Poppies, Foxgloves, annual Lupins and *Adonis autumnalis*.

Native plants were dug up in the wilds and re-planted in gardens, a practice that was much commoner than one might suppose. Our native Primroses, Cowslips, Cranesbills, Campions, Lychnis, Campanulas and Dianthus formed quite a large proportion of the inhabitants of gardens where little money could be spent in buying new plants.

It is in the variety of plants that we see a slowly awakening interest in horticulture. Many of those mentioned must have been unsuited to the formal garden and were relegated to the kitchen garden where their descendants are still amongst the most popular of plants. As time went on, old accounts show that owners of quite unpretentious gardens bought or exchanged each year a few Ranunculus and Tulips and seeds of double Marigolds, annual Lupins and Delphiniums. The desire for beauty in the garden was undoubtedly growing.

VEGETABLES.—Vegetables were grown both in quantity and in variety in a number of great gardens; yet travellers' references to the scarcity of vegetables throughout the country, except the universal Cole-wort or Kail, are so frequent that one is forced to believe them. Peas, Broad Beans, yellow Turnips and Beet Chard seem to have been the most popular, with, oddly enough, Asparagus becoming quite a common vegetable early in the eighteenth century, chiefly on the east coast where it grows well.

Among the accounts preserved at Dalkeith there is one of particular interest.[20] This is from a market gardener, John Arro, who supplied the house with vegetables from December 9, 1702, to September 14, 1703, while the garden at Dalkeith was being made. As it shows the length of time over which vegetables were in season the following list is given:

Artichokes	.	May to August
Asparagus	.	April to May
Beans .	.	July
Cabbage	.	December to February
Carrots	.	December to March, June to August
Cauliflowers	.	July
Cellary	.	December to March
Colewort	.	February to May
Lettuce	.	February to August
Onions	.	December, April to August
Peas .	.	July
Savoys	.	February to March
Scorzonera	.	February to May
Spinage	.	December to August
Turnips	.	December to February, June to August

In addition, there are Parsley, Balm, Sage, Peppermint, Thyme, Horse Radish, Rosemary and numerous herbs all the year round.

The most interesting item is Potatoes supplied 3 dozen at a time at 8s. to 12s. (Scots) on nine occasions between December and February, a very early date for Potatoes to have been supplied by a market gardener. They are mentioned by John Reid, and as early as 1697 they were suggested by an agricultural writer as excellent plants for growing in fields, but it was long before they became a popular article of diet and for many years they were sold in trifling quantities. Even as late as 1740 two sackfuls a day were sufficient for the requirements of the inhabitants of Paisley.

When Potatoes first began to creep into general cultivation, they were considered to be a tender plant. They were left in the ground from year to year, covered in the autumn with a thick blanket of bracken which was only removed when all danger of frost had disappeared. The main plant was left undisturbed and only the tubers growing round the edge were removed after the soil had been scraped carefully away. It was not until the second half of the century that they became popular, and not until near the end were they field-grown.

It is illuminating to compare two vegetable seed orders of the year 1720, one of Sir Robert Gordon of Gordonston,[24] a big landowner and a keen gardener, the other of a minister of an Ayrshire parish[70] who rode once a year to Edinburgh to attend the Church Assembly and rode back again with his small supply of garden seeds in his satchel. Unfortunately the quantities of the Gordonston order are not quoted, but it proves that large gardens were very well supplied and rather belies the statement in *The Social Life in Scotland in the Eighteenth Century* that vegetables were not served at table.

Sir Robert Gordon

Peas, eight varieties	Pompion and Gourd
Beans, three ,,	Cress
Radish, two ,,	Coucumer of severall sorts
Onions, two ,,	Melon
Turnip, two ,,	Purpie
Cabage, four ,,	Charvill
Letuce, three ,,	Smooth Spinage
Leeks	Shellot
Parsneep	Persly
Carrot	Clairie
Colliflower	Sumer and Winter Savory
Sweet-Majoram	Thym
Beetrave	Beet Chord
Cellery	

Minister

Ane ounce spinach	Ane ounce carrots
Ane ounce beetshard	2 ounce early turnips
½ ounce parsley	½ ane ounce yellow turnips
2 drms colliflower	1 lib turkey beans
2 drms lettuce	1 lib peas

FRUIT.—Although fruits of various kinds were by far the commonest of garden crops, only very few of the varieties grown at this period are even remembered by name; indeed, they show little variation on those grown in the monastic orchards, either in quality or in improved methods of cultivation. More efficient pruning may have been established since the Reformation and the value of various stocks more generally recognized, but the monks were much more thorough in the preparation of the ground and in the care which was exercised in planting: we rarely hear of the use of slabs of stone below the roots and the various layers of soil such as was commonly practised in the *pomaria* attached to most of the monasteries.

Visitors had little opinion of our tree fruit. Major wrote: "Orchards they have few. And their apples, pears and plumbs are not of the best kind; their cherries are tolerably good. And they have one sort of pear, large and well tasted, but seldom had. Wall fruit is very rare. But of gooseberries, currans, strawberries and the like, they have of each; but growing in gentlemen's gardens, and yet from thence we sometimes meet with them in the markets of their boroughs."[7]

The favourite fruit was still the Pear, which is so rarely grown with real success in Scotland to-day. It is true that many of the varieties were of the poorest quality, only fit for cooking, but it is probable that the quantity of Pears grown before 1730 was at least equal to all the other fruit trees added together. Descriptions of old orchards, particularly in the south, almost always emphasize the number of Pears grown. As a rule these consisted of the English Bergamot, Honey Pears, Bon Crètien, a number of Wardens, and a group of Scottish-raised Pears called Achans, with the Swann-egg and the Jargonelle gradually rising in favour.

Apples were next in popular esteem, although here again the quality must have been poor. The best dessert Apple was still the Golden Pippin beloved of Parkinson, "the greatest and best of all sorts of pippin", but the various Rennets and Russets were popular. There were also many varieties of native raising, among them the Arbroath Oslin, famous on the east coast since long before the Reformation, and a group of cooking Apples raised at, and called after, Leadington near Haddington, the Grey, Stoup, Green, White and Scarlet Leadington. Apples would have made more headway if cider had been drunk, but this was never a popular drink in Scotland.

Stone fruit was longer in coming into favour and was only seen in larger gardens. Cherries were the most popular, and of these the old Kentish, or Flanders, and the Morello were usually grown. Peaches and Apricots were much more uncommon, and so were Plums, of which the Mussel and the Imperial were sometimes seen. Sir John Foulis of Ravelston mentions the purchase of a "bona magna" Plum in his accounts for 1695.

Gooseberries and red and white Currants were common garden plants. As sugar was still expensive, little attempt was made at making preserves, but their wine was popular and frequent receipts exist on how to use both Gooseberries and Currants to best advantage. The Raspberry was still a comparatively rare fruit, but both white and red varieties were occasionally grown.

Very little is known of the early history of the Strawberry in Scotland. It was a popular fruit at an early date, but the wild Strawberry, *Fragaria vesca*, must have had a far wider distribution than it has now, and doubtless the berries so often mentioned were collected from wild plants. When cultivated forms were first grown in gardens is unknown, but in the description of the garden of Coltness in 1654 a Strawberry border is mentioned.

John Reid obviously appreciated them, for he gives detailed instructions about their cultivation. "Strawberries are a very fine and delicate fruit, and are easily increased, but best by the small plants taken from their mother plants at the strings in August, by which means they will be sufficiently rooted, so as not to be spued out of the ground by the frosts in winter. . . ." He advised growing the "great red strawberrie, and the Virginian, which is more early", both of which are mentioned in the five Strawberries in Tradescant's catalogue of 1656. In the Dalkeith accounts for 1702 there is one from a nursery gardener for a daily supply of Strawberries during the month of June. By the end of the seventeenth century its value as a fruit must have been fairly generally recognized.

CHAPTER IV

The National Type of Garden

1

The Country House and its Surroundings

By the third decade of the eighteenth century social conditions in Scotland were better. Trade was on the upgrade, and, with more money in the country, houses and estates were constantly being improved. Planting had not yet gained that impetus which reached its peak in the last few years of the century, when the "planting" Duke of Atholl was buying young trees by the million, but the number of plantations was sufficiently large to alter the face of the country. It was no longer a barren land where the traveller could pick out a few woods as worthy of comment. Hillsides were slowly being clothed, fields enclosed, lowlands drained and brought into cultivation; above all country houses, large and small, with their attendant policies, were being built or improved by landowners who were no longer satisfied with the discomfort and squalor to which their forebears were accustomed. It was the start of the agricultural age in Scotland, with its by-products of gardens, orchards and woods; and it is these which are of immediate concern to us.

The result of this desire for improvement was the

evolution at a rapid rate of the comfortable country estate for which Scotland is famous. Drumlanrig or Yester or Drummond Castle, magnificent though they may be, are not typical. Rather is it the house of moderate size, unpretentious in architecture, with its walled garden and nearby orchards, with its lawn shaded by fine trees, with its surrounding parks long laid out in grass, with its belts of timber sheltering the policies, the whole domain often surrounded by a stone wall: that is what is typical of a Scottish country house. The majority were built and the grounds laid out between 1735 and 1820.

You will note that this period commences at the same time as the pendulum began to swing in England from the formal to the picturesque, when Kent and his disciples of the landscape school started to sweep away much of the old. There was no such sudden change in Scotland; indeed, some of our formal gardens remained more or less unaltered, except in minor details, throughout the eighteenth century. Gilpin, who was imbued with the fashionable English hatred of the formal, toured the country in 1776. Many are his complaints of the formal gardens he saw, among them Hopetoun and Hamilton, but his chief criticism was left for Drumlanrig. After describing the beauties of the situation he continued: "It is amazing what contrivance hath been used to deform all this beauty". He spoke bitterly of canalizing the river and the existence of the great cascade. "So vile a waste of expense as this whole scene exhibits we rarely meet with. Deformity is spread wide through every part of it." [31] The scenery over

FIG. XII.—ROBERT ADAM'S DESIGN FOR A BRIDGE AT DALKEITH

which Gilpin waxed lyrical was very similar to that which inspired Burt, an officer of General Wade, to write not so many years before that "the huge naked rocks, being just above the heath, produce the disagreeable appearance of a scabbed head", the landscape being "a dismal brown drawing upon a dirty purple and most disagreeable of all when the heath was in flower". So tastes differ.

This survival of the formal garden was probably due to several causes: a natural dislike of wasting money by destroying what had formerly been considered well spent; our native conservatism; the fact that many of the great families were well content to stay at home as times improved. There was no sudden influx, such as occurred after the Restoration, of men returning to their estates filled with foreign ideas after years spent in exile. Many of the succeeding generation had been born in Scotland. Some possessed English estates and spent part of the year in the south; others again travelled little and were satisfied. Especially was this the case in Fife, Perthshire and Angus where the extreme type of landscape garden was rarely popular. Not only was there no sudden change in Scotland, but formal gardens continued to be made after their popularity had ceased in England. Hopetoun and Drumlanrig are examples; both were made on the formula of London and Wise about 1720.

Towards the end of the century, however, the landscape type of garden did begin to creep into the country, unfortunately in its most advanced and poorest forms. If it had kept to the modified and sensible type advised and practised by Lord Kames, our gardens would have been the better for it, but the usual "improver" was nothing but a poor imitator and plagiarist of "Capability" Brown in his most destructive mood. They ruined Glamis and a few more gardens north of the Forth, but did more damage in Midlothian and the Border country.

Henry Home, Lord Kames, wielded a great influence on Scottish agriculture and gardening. He was no armchair enthusiast, but worked as hard during his short visits to his estate at Blair Drummond as he did on the bench at the Court of Session. Whatever hour he reached home he went out to look at his garden and plantations, even if it meant carrying a lantern. He made one of the first landscape gardens at Blair Drummond about 1760 by planting an irregular ridge leading from the house with flowering shrubs and evergreens.

Very much to the point are his remarks on the purpose of the garden in his famous *Elements of Criticism*. He wrote that regularity was required in that part of a garden which was adjacent to the dwelling-house, but in proportion to the distance from the house regularity ought to be less and less considered.

This precept he carried out to the best of his ability at Blair Drummond. Unfortunately so much has been changed that little of the original garden remains. From what is known, it must have been a completely sensible garden. While he allowed regularity near the house, the more distant parts were never treated in the manner of the English landscape architects: they nearly approximated our ideas of a wild garden with walks wandering through woods which were partially gardened.

He was outspoken in his dislike of the affectations of the previous generations. "As gardening is not an inventive art, but an imitation of nature, or rather nature itself ornamented, it follows necessarily that everything unnatural ought to be rejected with disdain."[36] He had little use for topiary and "statues of wild beasts vomiting water", but allowed a whale spouting water from its head, as this was more or less of a natural phenomenon. This permission was followed by the profound truth that "the figure of a whale is in itself not agreeable".

The landscape garden only became a danger in Scotland when its popularity was on the wane in England, which probably accounted for the influx of itinerant garden designers of the utmost mediocrity who wandered through South Scotland trying to persuade landowners to employ them.

Luckily common sense found a doughty champion in Sir Walter Scott. He disliked extremes in gardens in any form, and was just as antagonistic towards Dutch topiary work as he was towards the advanced picturesque, while he approved of the formal garden of Italian style. "The distinction betwixt the Italian and Dutch is obvious. A stone hewn into a gracefully ornamented vase or urn has a value which it did not before possess; a yew hedge clipped into a fortification is only defaced. The one is a production of art, the other a distortion of nature."[68]

That he loved a beautiful garden is more than

proved by his well-known description of a house in which he once lived: "A small cottage, adjacent to a beautiful village, the habitation of an ancient maiden lady, was for some time our abode. It was situated in a garden of seven or eight acres, planted about the beginning of the eighteenth century by one of the Millers, related to the author of the *Gardeners' Dictionary*, or, for aught we know, by himself. It was full of long straight walks betwixt hedges of yew and hornbeam, which rose tall and close on every side. There were thickets of flowering shrubs, a bower, and an arbour, to which access was obtained through a little maze of contorted walks, calling itself a labyrinth. In the centre of the bower was a splendid Platanus, or oriental plane—a huge hill of leaves—one of the noblest specimens of that regularly beautiful tree which we remember to have seen. In different parts of the garden were fine ornamental trees which had attained great size, and the orchard was filled with fruit-trees of the best description. There were seats and trellis-walks, and a banqueting-house." [68] That is an admirable description of an eighteenth-century Scottish garden.

He goes on to express his disgust at improvements which he found on visiting it again after an absence of many years: "Its air of retreat, the seclusion which its alleys afforded, was entirely gone; the huge Platanus had died, like most of its kind, in the beginning of this century; the hedges were cut down, the trees stubbed up, and the whole character of the place so much destroyed that we were glad when we could leave it. This was the progress of innovation, perhaps of improvement: yet, for the sake of that one garden, as a place of impressive and solemn retreat, we are inclined to enter a protest against the hasty and ill-considered destruction of things which, once destroyed, cannot be restored." Improvements were obviously not confined to great gardens.

His chief scorn was kept for the disciples of Kent and "Capability" Brown: "For waterworks and architectural ornaments, the professed productions of art, Kent produced ha-has! sheets of artificial water, formal clumps and belts of trees, and bare expanded flats or slopes of shaven grass, which, indicating the recent use of the levelling spade and roller, have no more resemblance to that of nature which we desire to see imitated, than the rouge of an antiquated coquette, bearing all the marks of a sedulous toilette, bears to the artless blush of a cottage girl. His style is not simplicity, but affectation labouring to be simple."

Finally, let us look at his picture of a good-natured landlord in the toil of one of these gentry: "A pupil of Brown, Robertson by name, laid out the flat grounds of Duddingstone, near Edinburgh. The place was flat, though surrounded by many distinguished features. A brook flowed through the grounds, which, by dint of successive dam-heads, was arrested in its progress, twisted into the links of a string of pork-sausages, flung over a stone embankment, and taught to stagnate in a lake with islets, and swans *quantum sufficit*. It was to be expected that some advantage might have been gained by looking out from some point of the grounds on

Craigmillar Castle, a ruin beautiful in its form and interesting in its combinations with Scottish history; and the professor of landscape-gardening was asked, why so obvious a resource had not been made something of? He replied, with the gravity becoming such a character, that Craigmillar, seen over all the country, was a common prostitute. A less ludicrous, though equally nonsensical, reason for excluding Duddingstone Loch, a small and picturesque lake, was, that it did not fall within his lordship's property, and the mountain of Arthur's Seat was not excluded, only because it was too bulky to be kept out of sight. We have heard the excellent old Lord Abercorn mention these circumstances with hearty ridicule; but he suffered Mr Robertson to take his own way, because, he said, every man must be supposed to understand his own business, and partly, we may add, because he did not choose to take the trouble of disputing the point."

Duddingston was a famous example of the extreme type of landscape gardening, Even Loudon paused in his ponderous descriptions of gardens throughout the world to anathematize its treatment; but we could look upon Loudon's views with less suspicion if he had not made a serious suggestion of turning Arthur's Seat into a public promenade with a sprinkling of cemeteries, churches, chapels, monuments and public-houses.

The situations of large country houses and their surroundings were often such that there was little need for improvement of the landscape. At this period many houses were in existence in sites chosen for their beauty, where natural features supplied all the improvement necessary and it would have been almost sacrilege to allow the landscape architect a free rein. Monteviot with its lovely stretch of river, Floors Castle with its lawns sweeping down to the Tweed, Drumlanrig with its magnificent views towards the hills and its great woods, Keir with the vale of Stirling below, and so on.

Planting was sufficiently advanced to allow for countless miles of walks among woods and parks: at Dalkeith there were 50 miles of walks to keep up in 1812. The great stretches of policy woods surrounding these houses were far from uninteresting to landowners who were almost passionately addicted to planting. What could be more in keeping with the times than walks among these woods; and this habit was not confined to the great houses.

2

The Walled Garden

The most typical of the components of the Scottish estate is the walled garden. It is true that these exist in all parts of the British Isles, but nowhere in such numbers as in Scotland; nor is the use to which the kitchen garden is placed exactly the same in other parts of the country, except, perhaps, in the extreme north of England.

Through all the changes which have taken place in gardens and horticulture the walled garden has very largely kept its character and differs little from the original conception in the middle of the eighteenth century. It is still a very pleasant mixture of flowers, fruit and vegetables, a compact area enjoyed by the whole household and under the watchful eye of the gardener. Our forebears paid much attention to the kitchen garden, an attention worthy of respect which is still paid in Scotland.

The walled kitchen garden is usually at a distance from the house, often only a hundred or two yards but sometimes as much as half a mile. In houses and gardens built during the eighteenth century after the formal period it is rare to find the walled garden and the house as part and parcel of one architectural scheme. The reason most often given for the distance between house and garden is that the formal precision of straight paths and borders and rectangular vegetable plots was considered impossible by landscape architects. This may have been true in England but is less applicable in Scotland where gardens were much less under their influence. In large estates, where strictly formal gardens were laid out during the previous period in close proximity to the house, there was little room for the utilitarian rectangle surrounded with more or less unornamented walls, which, therefore, had to be made at a distance. Later, when a modified form of the informal near the house made wide lawns so popular under the windows, the walled kitchen garden again was hardly in keeping with the immediate surroundings of the house; but it was never treated with contempt, as was so common in England, and rigorously shut off out of sight of the house. Indeed, many which exist to-day are in full view.

FIG. XIII.—THE WALLED GARDEN AT CAMPERDOWN HOUSE, TYPICAL OF THE EARLY NINETEENTH CENTURY

It is a pity that Sir Walter Scott disliked the walled garden and was cruel in his criticism. Possibly it shows that he admired trees more than a garden; at any rate it proves that he missed the essence of the walled kitchen garden, the charming mixture in one enclosure of so much that is grown in gardens. He wrote: "It were indeed high time that some one should interfere. The garden, artificial in its structure, its shelter, its climate and its soil, which every consideration of taste, beauty, and convenience recommended to be kept near to the mansion, and maintained, as its appendage, in the highest state of ornamental decoration which could be used with reference to the character of the house itself, has, by a strange and sweeping sentence of exile, been condemned to wear the coarsest and most humbling form. Reduced to a clumsy oblong, inclosed within four rough-built walls, and sequestered in some distant corner where it may be best concealed from the eye to which it has been rendered a nuisance, the modern garden resembles nothing so much as a convict in his gaol apparel, banished, by his very appearance, from all decent society. If the peculiarity of the proprietor's taste inclines him to worship of Flora or Pomona, he must attend their rites in distance and secrecy, as if he were practising some abhorred mysteries, instead of rendering an homage which is so peculiarly united with that of the household gods."[68]

By the end of the century the walled kitchen garden, the lawns about the mansion, the shrubberies and the attendant policies were so common in the lowlands as to warrant their being called a national type of garden. The general lay-out followed no extremes either of formality or of the landscape type of garden architecture. From the aesthetic point of view it probably lacked the completeness that goes with a house and garden designed by one hand. Both house and garden were separate entities joined by no close ties of design; as such it might be imagined that they would be unsuited to further treatment, that the house would always remain the house and that the garden would always stand boxed off in its own watertight compartmnet. But that is not the case. This method of individual planning has suited the country admirably: it has formed a solid ground-work which has proved capable of infinite adjustment and infinite variety at the hands of gardeners of succeeding generations.

The very simplicity of the lay-out of most eight-eenth-century gardens and policies has proved a saving grace; there were no mannerisms which offended the sensibilities of the Victorian gardener with his meticulous bedding displays. In many cases the beds were carved out of the ample area of lawn, only to have the turf relayed when the popularity of the bedding craze ceased. Shrubberies have proved easily adaptable to hold the increasing number of varieties of flowering trees and shrubs. Wild gardens have been made from policy woods.

The modern gardener has to thank his forebears for the generous supply of lawn round the house. Rose gardens, flower gardens, water gardens, ter-races, these have all been constructed out of what was once an eighteenth-century lawn; and in most cases there is ample left over. When this has not been sufficient, the modern gardener has usually been able to encroach on the grass parks of the policies.

Through all these changes the walled kitchen garden has quietly held the premier place, unaltered and, really, unalterable. Of all forms of gardens it appears to be the solitary example which will not bear improvement except in details of cultivation. Its uses and appearance are very much the same to-day as they were two centuries ago.

The usual form has main paths running parallel to the walls and separated from them by borders about 8 feet wide. Two other main paths run through the middle of the garden at right angles to each other. With the advent of greenhouses they were often placed (the lean-to type) on the south side of the north wall. The amount of ground devoted to flowers depends on the individual taste of the owner, but there is usually a flower border or beds in front of the greenhouses, and almost always flower borders flanking the two main paths crossing the centre of the garden.

In the country home fashioned in the eighteenth century there is usually a pleasant and imperceptible shading from the cultivated garden to the parks and the policies. The Scottish laird used to live very close to the land; all the landscape he wanted was satisfied with his woods and his parks with his beasts fattening in them. There was no need for any elaboration; his lawns, whether closely scythed or left rough, as they often were, finished with a shrubbery or even with a plain paling, or more rarely with a ha-ha, if the lie of the land was suitable. The lawns round the house were unornamented except for specimen trees or a simple form of the parterre filled with common flowers. All architectural features were eschewed, except occasional ornamentation of the walls of the kitchen garden, and possibly a garden house.

Policies were often completely surrounded by a belt of trees. Critics have complained that this was one of the results of the landscape gardener: there may be a simpler explanation. Planting had taken a firm hold on the imagination of most landowners, planting both for future profit and for present shelter. Having discovered the benefits of planting, both real and supposed, they treated it as children will a new toy and overdid it. The same thing happened with garden walls. Some gardens still exist where the main kitchen garden is divided and subdivided by interior walls which were entirely unnecessary for the possible requirements of fruit. James Justice, writing in the middle of the century, advised those of his readers who considered they had too little walling to "divide your garden, with one or two walls through the middle of it, according to the size and extent of your ground".[39]

It is possible that the swing of the pendulum was not the sole cause for the complete change from the formal garden of the previous era. The formal garden relied largely for its effect on ornamentation other than flowers. Elaborate scrolls and arabesques were spoilt unless they were filled with plants of the same shape and size: conversely, many garden flowers looked out of place in the formal garden. Horticulture made great strides in Scotland once the old idea was swept away that most plants were not hardy in our more rigorous climate. Now that the garden flora was increasing so rapidly in variety, it was found that the shrubbery and the borders and beds of the kitchen garden suited most plants admirably. In a very short time not only the gardener but the laird and his family became flower lovers. It was natural to find that most herbaceous plants, bulbs and annuals grew best in the kitchen garden where the soil was better tilled and better fed.

In the north the same process of evolution was clearly seen, particularly on the shores of the Moray Firth, where country houses with their attendant policies and gardens sprang up on every side. At the beginning of the nineteenth century their general excellence was such that they had to be cast on a very large scale to attract attention and description.

3

Garden Practice

Horticultural practice improved as gardens increased in number. Owners were no longer satisfied with the old rough and ready methods of cropping as much as possible from land that was sour, unmanured and in poor heart. It was the start of the golden age of Scottish horticulture; in the short space of a hundred years our gardeners from a humble beginning brought our garden practice to a pitch of excellence that was not excelled even in the great gardens of England.

It must be remembered that we lacked the ground-work of centuries on which to build up our knowledge; we had no experience that was passed on from generation to generation, no equivalents of Tusser, Hill, Mascall, Platt, Gerard, Markham, Lawson, Parkinson, Austen, Meager or Evelyn to teach us a little about plants and something of the gardener's cunning: only one unknown man, John Reid, was bold enough to point out the way in print before 1750.

Some few great gardens were started before the commencement of the eighteenth century, but they were probably controlled by that class of professional gardener who, though Scottish by extraction, seemed to have ruled many of the large English gardens. They would not be tempted away from comfortable positions to return to a country just awakening from acute poverty unless their new domain was of the largest size. The average laird had to fend for himself and rely on local talent; it was the native gardener who proved himself so adaptable and quick to learn from his own experience.

Before the eighteenth century was old, a few, a very few, of our horticulturists were sufficiently advanced for their names to be known outside their own country. One was Andrew Heron of Bargully in Kirkcudbrightshire, who, when visiting a gardener near London to whom he was a stranger, astonished his host by his botanical knowledge. On Heron naming a rare exotic his host is said to have remarked, "Then, sir, you must either be the devil, or Andrew Heron of Bargully".[44] He was one of the first specialists in Scotland, among his favourite plants being variegated Hollies and autumn-flowering Crocuses.

It was not until 1754 that John Reid's book was superseded by a more modern work, James Justice's *The Scots Gardener's Director*.[39] But, notwithstanding the lack of horticultural literature, knowledge was being spread by keen landowners who realised that improved cultivation was as important in gardens as in agriculture and who were not ashamed to learn from every possible source. Among these improvers was John Cockburn of Ormiston, whose *Letters to his Gardener*[17] from 1727 to 1744 were published by the Scottish History Society in 1904.

As a Lord of the Admiralty much of Cockburn's active life was spent in London. On his retirement Ormiston unfortunately had to be sold and was purchased by the Hopetoun family. Thus it was usually by precept and advice from a distance that Cockburn was able to influence the community of his East Lothian estate. He was whole-heartedly in favour of long leases and did much in his neighbourhood to break down the pernicious system of yearly tenancies. This produced protracted legislation, as his leases were contested and were only sustained by the House of Lords as late as 1865.

These long leases, however, removed a common cause of complaint, that it was never worth a tenant's

while improving his land. It was only after security
of tenure was assured that the soil could be properly
cultivated and that more permanent improvements,
such as planting of fruit trees and hedges or making
walls, could be undertaken. As the gradual increase
of the years of tenancy coincided more or less with
improved prices for agricultural products, it was not
long before the general standard of living was raised
throughout the country.

Some of Cockburn's letters deal with the gardening
prowess of his gardener's father, a stubborn old Scot.
In one, dated 1735, he wrote: "This I design chiefly
for some thoughts about Improving of your father's
garden and land of which if you do right you'l turn a
good deal off into Kitchen and Orchard Garden. In
doing of which I still think you might have made
more progress last winter and by so doing you might
have made a beginning in drawing in the people to a
better taste towards Garden stuff. . . . I can't think
the finding of the ground was a full excuse, for tho'
the cleaning of much at once might have been expensive, yet I can't think but the cleaning and putting
some in order had it only been to introduce what I
am sure by good management, you'l find advantage
in afterwards, would have been for your service.
Indeed if you propose to follow your father's narrow,
vastly mistaken notion of raising ten cabbages and
not disposing of them, tho' in danger of rotting,
unless he gets the price of thirty, you'l be in the
right, provided nobody will raise cabbages but your-
self, but this wont hold long, for the dearer you keep
up the price the more others will be encouraged to

take up the business, which is the constant consequence of those foolish, narrow, low notions. A man
in a fortnight or three weeks would have trenched as
much as would have made a beginning and would
have paid for the trouble and have increased the
demand next year, besides the advancing a year of
such small or large fruits as you had planted. Your
father's garden is well sheltered by the houses and
rising ground from the one hand and by the high
hedge of the other, and he has water at hand. So he
may raise anything in it the climate will allow of. He
has crowded it with fruit trees, too thick even for
them to bear as they would, especially when a little
older, as in that warm place they advance very fast.
By this he loses the undergrowth also by which he
might make double crops for a kitchen or if for fruit
which would answer as well in the most exposed part
of his field. So warm a lying spot should either have
been employed entirely in double crops for a kitchen
or if for fruit it should have been in kinds every spot
wont produce, and for that reason yielded more."[17]

That shows excellently the kind of homely advice
given on garden matters by an "improving" landlord
to his servants and tenantry.

The new owners of Ormiston made great improvements in the gardens during the following hundred
years. At the beginning of the nineteenth century it
was famous for the varied collections of plants it
contained; over 500 different herbaceous plants, 110
shrubs, 270 varieties of Roses, 70 or 80 different
annuals and many bulbs.

The greatest influence on garden practice during

this period was James Justice. He was a remarkable man, well educated, who had travelled much in Holland and France. He was a Clerk of the Court of Session and a Fellow of the Royal Society. He was also a very skilled gardener, and his garden, close to Edinburgh, was famous for its collections of rare plants. He had a fine conceit, but those who wish to take the trouble to read his admirable book should not be put off by his grandiloquent style. In the preface to the first edition he starts: "I have studied and practised gardening in every part of it, for these 30 years bypast; I have satisfied the most learned societies in Britain, of my practice and knowledge in the Culture of the nicest flowers, and of plants both exotick and indigenous, which adorn our British gardens, and have been highly honoured by them upon that account. I have been a long time importuned to publish my practice in gardening, which, with the persuasion that it is my duty to serve my country to the utmost of my power, induced me to yield to the importunities of many and prepare this treatise for the press." [17] Nevertheless, even with such a beginning, it is a very good book.

Justice gives no instructions on the designing of ornamental gardens, but details fully the kitchen garden with its complement of vegetables, fruit and flowers. So minute are his instructions about situation, exposure, walls, frames and hot beds and so exactly do they describe many old extant gardens that either his precepts must have been carried out on many estates, or he must have been citing as examples gardens already in existence.

102

FIG. XIV.—THE CHARACTERISTIC BOX-EDGED PARTERRE AT DALZELL.

John Reid was so thorough in what he wrote about actual manual labour that it could scarcely be improved. One practice, however, disappeared, first from large gardens and then by degrees from smaller, the system of ridging. Common sense told the gardener that this held no possible benefit.

The most important change during this period was in the use of walls. They had, of course, been seen for over a century and a half in Scottish gardens; the difference lay in the fact that in the past they had combined utility with their existence as architectural features. Any architectural pretensions now disappeared entirely and in their place came the purely utilitarian aspect of sheltering plants.

From the many pages that Justice devoted to walls in all their aspects it is obvious that they played a very large part in eighteenth-century garden technique. He began by advising their orientation a few degrees east of south. As he gardened on the east coast, he must have been aware of the danger of early sunshine striking fruit blossoms after a night of spring frost; but he gave that direction as his definite opinion, and said that the advantages of better ripening in autumn more than outweighed possible loss caused by frosting in the spring. He disliked walls built on a curve and said that they proved to be frost traps.

Most walls of this period were made of stone, rough dressed on the outside and set with mortar. Brick was rare in Scotland before the nineteenth century. Defoe drew attention to this scarcity. He described how he saw bricks being made for the wall

103

round the garden at the Marquess of Annandale's house near Queensferry, "a thing hardly to be seen in Scotland, except there".[21] In some parts of the country where rock was easily split dry walls were not uncommon. Sometimes walls were arched at intervals at the base. Fruit trees planted opposite these arches were supposed to benefit by the extension of their roots through the arch to a cooler north exposure. Similar arches are occasionally seen in boundary walls in fields.

There was one class of wall that was common in Scotland from the middle of the eighteenth century until about 1825; that was the hot wall. This method of forcing fruit had been practised in England before 1720, but it was a simple system of heating the backs of walls at intervals by means of ovens. Later, in 1732, a hollow wall was made at Knowsley Hall near Liverpool in which a fire was lighted on cold nights. The system advocated by Justice was an advance on the latter. Furnaces were built at intervals below ground-level at the back of the wall, but instead of the wall being hollow throughout, where the supply of a sufficient draught must have been a difficulty, a system of flues was built in the wall, branching out from a central chamber above the furnace and running at various angles to the top of the wall. Tests made lately on a hot wall, where the flues and furnace had been cleaned out, show that a sufficient temperature must have been generated to keep off a fairly severe frost; but the size of the furnace, whether it burned wood or coal, was not sufficient to maintain an equal temperature for many hours on end. This must have been a distinct drawback.

These hot walls were used for forcing Grapes, Peaches and Nectarines. Lean-to lights, glazed either with glass or more rarely oiled paper, were kept in position from February until danger from spring frosts was over. They leant against the wall at the top while their base rested on a narrow foundation five feet away from the wall. Justice advised that only one-third of the area of hot wall should be utilized each year, thus resting the vines and fruit trees for two years out of every three. In his day it was universally believed that forcing every year was injurious to the plants. Later Peaches and Nectarines were forced every year, but Vines were cropped two years and then left fallow for three, a strict rotation of five years.

The remains of these flued walls still exist in a number of Scottish gardens; they are most commonly met with in Angus, Fife and Midlothian

Justice was a most successful cultivator of fruit. While utilizing all available wall space he much approved of the use of espaliers, especially for Apples, Pears, Plums, Cherries and Currants; for the last he also advocated a north wall.

It is unfortunate that so little is known of the early history of the greenhouse, although it is only natural, as old examples were usually destroyed with the great advance that took place in greenhouse construction during the last century. It is usually stated that Duilhier and Switzer are responsible for the idea of the greenhouse, as opposed to the heated room or orangery of the seventeenth century. Switzer certainly adapted the hot wall and in place of movable lean-to lights built erections with a permanent roof and supporting pillars with three tiers of openings between each pillar for sashes of glass which were removed during summer.

It is possible that the greenhouse in Scotland originated by a process of enlargement from the Melon frame. These were certainly in fairly general vogue by 1720, for the advantage of confining heat raised by means of a hot-bed must soon have been realized. The next stage was the pit for Pineapples. It is known that Justice was the first man to ripen this fruit in Scotland, about 1750, and from that date they increased rapidly in numbers. Dr. Patrick Neill, in writing of greenhouses, said: "They are sometimes of the same construction as pine-stoves; sometimes they are merely houses furnished with large upright windows, with narrow pillars between them, and roofed with slates; and sometimes they are many-sided figures, glazed on all their sides, and the roof terminating in a point, glazed to the summit. This last form seems best adapted for the health of the plants."[54]

Hot walls with their movable lean-to lights were in common use long after vineries and hothouses were standard essentials in all large Scottish gardens. So much is this the case that Neill stated quite definitely in his Government report on *Scottish Gardens and Orchards*, published in 1812, that "hot walls are chiefly used for the raising of peaches and nectarines; but in some few instances, apricots and figs are also placed on them. It must be admitted, that in Scot-

FIG. XV.—AN OLD TYPE OF GREENHOUSE WITH SLIDING ROOF LIGHTS

land, hot walls are highly important, if not absolutely necessary, for the perfect production of the two former."[54]

As has been remarked before, permanent structures erected in front of hot walls never attained much success in Scotland. Although the type of building was the same with straight fronts and a roof made of tiles or lead, yet they were always supplied with an oven or flues inside the building and not confined in the walls. In most cases the sashes were either removable or slid up and down like an ordinary window.

Apparently one of the first greenhouses of the lean-to type, as we now know it, was built at Scone by the head gardener, a Mr Beattie, about 1806. This was considered at the time a great novelty, as the roof swept down to within 2 feet of the ground; and, in addition, it was possibly the first time that fixed glass with ventilators at top and bottom was seen in Scotland. Greenhouses of this date were often glazed with narrow panes rounded at the base to let the drip run off freely. Another innovation was the use of earthenware flues, circular in section, in shape like an elongated chimney-can. Heating by steam or water did not begin before 1829.

The first greenhouse to be used in the nursery trade in Scotland belonged to Leslie in Edinburgh and was erected about 1770.

Hothouses must have been far from satisfactory owing to the drying influence on the air of the application of direct heat by means of flues. Various expedients were used to try to circumvent this fault, of which the most satisfactory was tanner's bark. This was allowed to ferment and so kept the air moist to a certain extent. It proved most successful in Pineapple pits, where it was largely used.

Considering the difficulties it is amazing to what a degree of skill gardeners of the day reached not only in forcing fruit but also in growing greenhouse plants, such as Cape Heaths, of which the technique is considered extraordinarily difficult to-day, even with our improved appliances.

Another element of garden practice in which eighteenth-century gardeners excelled was the hot-bed. They were certainly in use in the seventeenth century and are mentioned by John Reid, while Cockburn was fully aware of their value about 1730; but it remained for Justice to collect all the known information on the subject and describe it in detail. Hot-beds were made in the open and also under frames and large bell glasses. The heating medium was usually stable manure. Hot-beds were used principally for forcing early vegetables and to a lesser extent fruit. So skilful were some gardeners in this technique that it was possible to see Mushrooms on the table throughout the winter, forced Asparagus by the end of December, Cucumbers by the beginning of March, and Peas and Beans by the end of March.

For forcing fruit the hot-bed was made up at the back of a tall and solid wooden paling on which the trees were trained. In frosty weather a lean-to light was used as in the case of hot walls. Peaches, Nectarines and Grapes were forced by this method, and also Strawberries, which were planted in front of the fruit trees close enough to be covered by the lights.

It is possible to gain a very fair idea of the cost of working a great garden—that at Dalkeith—in the year 1812, as the exact size is known and, in addition, all the garden accounts for that year have been preserved. Dalkeith at this date was probably the largest garden in Scotland. Some information about its appearance 120 years before will be found in the previous chapter. Since that date it had undergone numerous alterations and enlargements. The large kitchen garden and the orchard were made about 1760, but the ground had been insufficiently prepared and for many years they had been extremely unproductive. An immense amount of subsoil was removed and fresh soil spread in its place shortly after 1800. In 1812 the kitchen garden and orchard covered 13 Scots acres. There was in addition a garden 500 feet long by 40 broad devoted to the cultivation of rare plants of all kinds, an alcoved walk for climbers and a flower garden near the house. The houses and frames consisted of:

Two vineries,	50 ft. by	17 ft.
Stove,	40 ft. ,,	17 ft.
Rose house,	30 ft. ,,	12 ft.
Conservatory	52 ft. ,,	21 ft.
Greenhouse,	40 ft. ,,	17 ft.
Melon ground,	400 ft. ,,	50 ft. containing 60 frames

Over 1000 different herbaceous plants were grown. In addition, the head gardener, James McDonald, used to carry out a great deal of propagating in the gardens. Between 2000 and 3000 fruit grafts were made each year. These were used in a curious fashion. Instead of replacing old fruit trees in the kitchen garden and orchard McDonald used to graft several fresh varieties, using the old trees as stocks. From five to eight different sorts were often grafted on the same tree, with, apparently, excellent results.

For this great garden the accounts from November 7, 1812, to November 6, 1813, worked out as follows:

	£	s.	d.
Garden Wages:			
James McDonald, Head Gardener, paid £44 half yearly	88	0	0
3 foremen @ 2s. per day . . .			
13 journeymen @ 1s. 10d. per day . .			
4 ditto @ 1s. 8d. per day . . .			
1 ditto @ 1s. 6d. per day . . .			
1 apprentice @ 1s. 1d. per day .			
3 ditto @ 1s. per day			
2 ditto @ 6d. per day			
15 women weeders @ 9d. per day . .			
(17 of these could not write and made their mark, most of the women among them.)			
Total for the year .	749	11	6
6 Labourers paid from 1s. 4d. to 2s. per day:			
Total for the year .	138	18	0
3 Carters paid from 1s. 6d. to 2s. per day:			
Total for the year .	80	12	0
Plants and Seeds:			
Dicksons and Co.	42	8	0
James Scougall	8	3	0
William Ballantyne . . .	22	3	5
Sundries:			
Edinburgh Glasshouse Co.—glass .	36	5	9
The Blind Asylum—331 yards of net . .	5	12	6
William Creelman—flower pots . . .	4	11	0
George Gordon—ditto . . .	22	17	6

	£	s.	d.
Wilson and Elliott—flooring nails	1	18	8
John Crouch—fruit baskets	1	10	0
William Shiells—garden tools, wall nails, &c.	26	4	5
Alexander McDonald—tinsmith	5	10	10
John Cream—tanners bark	2	2	0
Walter Smith—saddlery and leather for gardens	10	7	7
John Gray—oil for gardens	1	6	3
William Skiddon—medicine for horses	0	5	0
George Blackie—plumbing works in gardens	38	0	5
Gardener's disbursements	37	12	0

Giving a total for the year of . £1323 19 10

4

Plants

Our garden flora changed little until the century was well advanced. The end of the old floral era which had commenced in Elizabethan days was approaching, and we can find but little difference between most of the flowers suggested by John Reid in 1683 and those catalogued in 1750. During the two previous centuries there had been new introductions from abroad, principally from the two Americas, but few of them had become really popular as garden plants.

Plant breeding and selection, except in a few instances such as the Auricula, were rarely practised in Scotland before 1770, and were really not understood, with the consequence that material used to fill flower-beds and borders was not of great quality.

111

We may wax enthusiastic over old-fashioned plants, but many of those on which we look with such pride only date from a hundred, or at the most a hundred and fifty, years ago. We have only to examine illustrations of garden flowers prior to 1750 to admit, if we are honest, that most of them would be unworthy of a place in the modern garden.

Contemporary seed and plant catalogues were notoriously suspect as regards correct nomenclature and the quality of their material; so gardeners as a rule were satisfied with the popular varieties of former generations. Perennials were propagated as far as possible by division or cuttings, while annuals and biennials were often grown from home-saved seed; instructions for their harvesting were common in gardening literature of the time: "Gather the seeds of such flowers as you intend to sow afterwards; as those of Auriculas, Polyanthos &c, preserving them in the pods, by putting the pods into blowing Flower-glasses, and exposing them to the sun in a place sheltered from rain for a month or so, when they may be rubbed out".[67]

Sir Herbert Maxwell describes an old tapestry at Monreith made before 1771, in which is shown a bouquet, and a very charming one, of the popular garden flowers of the day: Madonna and Isabelline Lilies, Clove Carnation, Mullein, Hyacinth, Red Primrose, Auricula, Polyanthus, Guelder Rose, Anemone, Moss Rose, Scarlet Lychnis, Pink Geranium, Convolvulus, Sunflower, Sweet William, Scabious, Canterbury Bell and the double Butter and Egg Daffodil.[51] This may be taken as a good sample of the inhabitants of an ordinary flower garden of the middle of the century.

A few new annuals and biennials began to be grown before the middle of the century, such as the China Aster and the Indian Pink, but the greatest increase in the numbers of varieties was certainly in bulbs. This trade was a monopoly of Dutch nurserymen, who issued long lists of names, too long even for Justice, who complained of the number of varieties of extraordinary similarity. By degrees many varieties of Colchicum, Crocus, Tulip, Anemone, Ranunculus, Lily, Hyacinth, Crown Imperial and Narcissus began to spread through the country, and there were few gardens that did not provide an excellent show of bulbous flowers, probably in greater variety than annuals or perennials.

Ornamental trees and shrubs were increasing in number and variety, particularly towards the end of the century, when more natural planting became fashionable. At the start they were limited to white, mauve and purple Lilacs, one or two Spiraeas, the Guelder Rose, the Mock Orange and the Laburnum, with the single and double Gean, *Prunus Avium*, still first favourite among flowering trees. Later one or two of the St. John's Worts and the white Broom, *Cytisus albus*, were extensively grown, while at the beginning of the nineteenth century American shrubs, such as Arbutus, Kalmias and Azaleas, had a great vogue, and "American Gardens" were frequently made on larger estates. In a very short time Heaths of various kinds and *Ericaceae* from other parts of the world were grown in "American Gardens", but

I

the name has survived in a remarkable fashion, so much so that in many catalogues of old-fashioned firms there is still a section devoted to American Plants, although by far the greater proportion come from Europe and Asia. Herbaceous borders were to be seen in most walled gardens long before the end of the century, only to be swept away during the Victorian era when gardeners disapproved of their picturesque informality.

Popular varieties of Roses were grown in almost all gardens, but strangely little enthusiasm was shown in Scotland until near the end of the eighteenth century. The first group of Scottish raised Roses was probably the Ayrshire Rose, which appeared at Loudon Castle in Ayrshire about 1770, and was first known as the Orangefield Rose. A little later it was distributed by Ayrshire nurserymen, and such was its popularity within a few years that it was generally known as the Ayrshire Rose.[27] About 1800 there appeared on the market the first hybrids of the Scots Rose, *Rosa spinosissima*, which caught the public fancy to a remarkable degree. During the first few decades of the last century these hybrids were certainly the most popular Roses in Scotland.

The policies which were planted round almost every house of any size during this period usually consisted of the commoner hardwoods with a few Scots Pine and common Spruce and a large number of Yews and Hollies to break the monotony of leafless boughs during the winter.

Exotic trees and plants in general began to creep into common cultivation before the end of the cen-

FIG. XVI.—THE AMERICAN GARDEN AT DRUMLANRIG, FROM A PHOTOGRAPH TAKEN IN 1902

tury: in fact, it is probably true that the hardy garden flora contained many more species and varieties in common use in 1800 than it did 60 years later at the height of the Victorian bedding craze.

It is interesting to note that Scotland had what was probably the first syndicate in the British Isles who paid collectors abroad for seeds. In the year 1765 a Society for Importation of Foreign Seeds was formed in Edinburgh under the leadership of the Professor of Botany, Dr. John Hope.[67] Little is known of its membership except that the Earl of Loudon was prominent; nor do we know anything of the results of the collections in this country, except that there is a possibility that the first Ayrshire Roses originated from Rose seed sent home from Quebec. Subscriptions were two guineas or more. In the first year three collections were imported, one from Quebec, 103 different species from Carolina and 115 different trees and shrubs from Philadelphia. A suggestion was made to send a collector to New-foundland, which did not materialise, but in 1768 a further collection of seed was sent from Quebec. This was collected by a Mr Wright, who styled himself a "collector of seeds". The list may be of some interest as showing the kind of trees of which the seed was imported,[67] and is printed in Appendix B.

The poor quality of most of the hardy garden flowers prior to 1800 was probably a reason for the extreme popularity of greenhouse plants which started before the end of the eighteenth century and continued for over a hundred years. It is difficult to believe that owners of gardens, however wealthy they may have been, would have gone to such trouble and expense growing plants under glass if there had been real quality in hardy plants. Tropical plants arrived, as it were, ready made in more brilliant colourings and with more opulent beauty, which made the ordinary garden flora look rather drab and dowdy.

The eighteenth century saw the commencement of an era of plant cultivation which has never been excelled, particularly when we realize that houses and heating arrangements were crude and that science had not yet stirred to lend a hand in horticulture and in combating plant diseases.

One of the earliest collections of hot-house plants in Scotland was that of Andrew Heron of Bargully, who grew in a hot room Oranges, Lemons, Pomegranates, Passion Flowers, Oleanders and Myrtles as early as 1720. It would be interesting to learn just how successful he may have been with these sun-loving plants.

The first greenhouse plant to achieve popularity was the Tuberose, which was quite common before the middle of the century. They were sold by almost all seedsmen, who imported them from Italy by way of London. The usual practice was to grow them on the hot-beds of Melon frames; when growth began, they were lifted with a ball of soil and two bulbs were potted in a "twopenny" pot when they were brought into the house to flower.

By the end of the century most gardens of any size could boast of their collections of greenhouse exotics, among which *Richardia africana*, *Gloriosa superba*, *Eucomis nana* and *E. striata*, the three Coronillas,

116

C. glauca, *C. juncea* and *C. valentina*, Heliotrope, *Poinsettia pulcherrima* and Oranges were usually prominent. A garden became famous for some special plant with which the gardener was particularly successful: at Woodhall about 1830 there was a wonderful specimen of *Cereus speciosissima* which filled over 250 square feet of wall and had 300 to 400 blooms in flower at the same time; another was proud of a 25-foot *Doryanthus excelsa*; Drummond Castle could boast of flowering an *Agave americana* in an ordinary greenhouse, a giant of a plant 23 feet high with 29 flowering branches and an average of 89 flowers on each branch, making 2581 flowers in all.[66]

One of the favourite indoor plants was the Cape Heath, which reached the height of its popularity early in the nineteenth century. Special houses were often built for them, including those at Moncreiff House and Eglinton Castle, where more than 900 plants in 200 species were cultivated. It was not uncommon to find plants of such species as *E. retorta* more than 5 feet in diameter, outgrowing the largest pots and planted in tubs.

Other plants were grown for indoor decoration. Acacias and Banksias were popular, and so were the numerous varieties of cut-leaved Geraniums. For a time Mignonette was extremely common as an indoor plant and was grown all the year round. It was trained in many forms, tree fashion, bush-, pyramid- and umbrella-shaped. When grown for size, it was usually sown in May and trained on wires; specimens were shown over 4 feet high by $2\frac{1}{2}$ feet in diameter.

An interesting outcome of the numerous introduc-

tions from abroad was the realization that the climate
of Scotland was not so desperate as was generally
imagined. In various areas tests were made of the
hardiness of these introductions. On the outskirts of
Edinburgh John Street, gardener to Mrs Hamilton
Nisbet of Beil, was famous for his experiments, while
we hear of *Leptospermum baccatum*, one or two of the
Acacias, and Myrtles surviving a winter outside in
Fife, and of *Eccremocarpus scaber*, *Passiflora coerulea*
and *Fuchsia coccinea*, *F. conica*, *F. gracilis*, *F.
virgata* being tried outside at Kelso, and apparently
passing the test.[66]

VEGETABLES.—There is nothing in the history of
Scottish gardening so puzzling as the relative importance of vegetables in the diet of the average Scot.
In previous chapters it has been shown that there is
sufficient proof that vegetables played a very small
part as late as the early seventeenth century. After
that there is sufficient evidence to prove that they
were much more grown than is usually stated. Even
as late as 1780 Wesley wrote: "When I was in
Scotland first (in 1762), even at a nobleman's table
we had only flesh meat of one kind, and no vegetables of any kind". It is only fair to him to say that
he qualified that by adding, "but now (in 1780) they
are as plentiful here as in England". Wesley was a
careful and just commentator, but it is quite impossible to believe that such a radical and sudden change
could have taken place in the short space of eighteen
years.

Apart from evidence given in the last chapter,
there is more than sufficient to prove that vegetables

of many kinds were not only known but skilfully cultivated in many parts of Scotland before the middle of the eighteenth century. There are numerous instances in Cockburn's *Letters* of reproof given to his gardener for not growing enough or for being unsuccessful, written in a note of surprise as if the gardener knew as well as his master about their successful cultivation. "Dont fall short in Onions and Leeks this year as you have commonly done. Get me plenty and good things for the Kitchen. You can now guess of what kinds the greatest demands are." [17]

Justice also wrote as if most vegetables were commonly known, although the average gardener often neglected to buy the best varieties. He mentions among others 7 kinds of Onion, 7 Turnips, 12 Lettuces, 5 Cucumbers, 10 Cabbages and 24 Peas. He would not describe them in such detail unless they were generally appreciated. Not only that but more uncommon vegetables are to be found both in seedsmens' lists and in gardeners' accounts. One comes across Scorzonera, Garlick, Sorrel, Endive, Celeriac, Gourd, Salsify, Skirret, Shallot, Rockambole, Chervil and Cardoon. Leeks, Asparagus, Radishes, Carrots and Beets were popular, while Broccoli and Cauliflower were coming more into fashion. Potatoes by the middle of the eighteenth century were a staple crop. A typical invoice for the yearly supply of garden seeds about 1820 is given in Appendix C.

The following table is given as a sample of rotation of crop (the dates are those of sowing or planting):

119

1793. Subtrenched; carrots; winter fallowed.
1794. Early Cauliflower, with moderate dunging, 2nd March; Yellow Turnip, with compost dressing, 20th July.
1795. Onions, without manure, 8th February; Cabbage, with light dunging, 5th October.
1796. Peas for a late crop, without manure, 10th June; trenched 3 spits deep in December; winter fallowed.
1797. Potatoes, with moderate dunging, 20th March; German Greens, without manure, 10th September.
1798. Leeks in June.

While at the start of the century vegetables were probably only appreciated in comparatively few houses where the owner and his family had learnt their value in England or abroad, by the end they were universally grown, and, oddly enough, often in greater variety than we are accustomed to now.

FRUIT.—If grumbles were still to be heard in the middle of the eighteenth century of the quality and quantity of vegetables, every traveller was enthusiastic about the abundance of fruit he found throughout the country. Fruit, indeed, was grown in enormous quantities in hothouses, kitchen gardens and orchards, both public and private. The orchards of Clydesdale and the Carse of Gowrie were particularly famous.

From the universal approbation we are forced to believe either that our climate has since changed for the worse, at least as far as the cultivation of fruit is concerned, or, as is more probable, that in those days people were satisfied with mediocre quality, while the importation of fruit is now so easy and so cheap that the immense amount of trouble taken to bring fine fruit to maturity is now no longer worth while. Whatever may be the reason, Scotland has to a great extent lost its reputation for tree fruit. One reason is possibly that old trees of poor varieties were allowed to remain in garden and orchard long past their climacteric: by 1812 over 100 varieties of Apple and 65 varieties of Pear were more or less commonly grown in Scotland, the vast proportion of which were worthless rubbish, long exceeded in quality and cropping by newer varieties.

At Dalkeith in 1810 there was one of the finest and most modern collections. This consisted of 28 different Apples, 20 Pears, 7 Cherries, 13 Peaches, of which 8 were grown outside, 9 Nectarines, of which only one was grown outside, 5 Apricots, all outside, 11 Plums and 2 Figs.

By the beginning of the nineteenth century the commonest of the better class varieties to be found in Scotland were:

Apples: Nonpareil, Ribston Pippin, Golden and Royal Russets.
Pears: Jargonelle, Beurre de Roy, Crasanne and St. Germain.
Plums: Green Gage, Golden Drop and Magnum Bonum.
Cherries: Mayduke and Kentish, also Morello.
Peaches: Early Newington, Red Nutmeg, Red Magdalen.
Nectarines: Elruge, Fairchild's Early.
Grapes: Black Hamburg, White Muscat of Alexandria, Black
  ditto, Royal Muscadine, White Sweetwater.

Of bush fruit Gooseberries and Currants were most often grown. A little later Scotland shared with England the Gooseberry craze, where individual fruits reached preposterous sizes. Raspberries were little grown or appreciated until the nineteenth century. Earlier Cockburn suggested in a letter to his gardener that some might be grown for distilling into brandy. This neglect of the Raspberry was curious, as modern practice has shown that it is an excellent crop in the midlands of Scotland. Strawberries also lagged behind in popularity. In the eighteenth century their value seemed to be as forced fruits, although several market gardeners near Edinburgh specialized in them and they appeared to find a ready market. Justice mentioned three varieties, the Virginian or Scarlet, the Globe Hautboy and the Greenish-white or Pineapple. By 1800 the Chile Strawberry was grown and conditions changed, for after that it became a very popular fruit. The first Scottish raised variety was called the Roseberry: it was bred in Aberdeen about 1810.

CHAPTER V

The Victorian Garden

WE have seen how gardening in Scotland had progressed so rapidly that by the end of the Georgian
period our gardens were little inferior to those in
England. From now on the history of gardening in
the two countries really cannot be separated. The
parish minister of Abercairney, near Crieff, described
the demesne as "a magnificent park, embellished
with the enchanting eye of imitating nature, in which
extensive lawns salute the eye, the antique alley,
venerable oaks, clumps and trees scattered in a lavish
style of sylvan beauty, whose dark shades serve as
foils to set off the lovelier mantle of the verdant
surface. No bold features of mountains, and rocks
and cascades, no wild misshapen forms, no grotesque
shapes constitute the beauty of the landscape. Nature
is here arrayed, in gentle attire, in the softer charms
of beauty united with utility; rich meadows, pleasing
acclivities, gardens enamelled with flowers, artificial
islands and lakes; and every hortulane and rural
decoration, essential to an elegant and commodious
residence."[66] Such grandiloquent descriptions were
as common in Scotland as in England during this
period; but the one quoted is a masterpiece, which

123

might have come from the pages of Thomas Love Peacock. Beneath the torrent of words one can sense a very pleasant and peaceful place; but it would apply to Headlong Hall equally as well as to Abercairney.

It is common to-day to run down most aspects of Victorian gardening; yet it had many good points. The quality of fruit reached an extremely high level; in the flower garden meticulous regard was paid to cultivation, and thousands of plants, as alike as two peas, were used each year in those massive bedding displays so beloved during the Victorian age; above all, gardeners were successful in bringing to maturity many species of tropical and sub-tropical genera which are rarely seen and still more rarely brought to perfection to-day. The popularity of greenhouse exotics which began in the closing years of the former century reached a triumphant climax in the middle of the Victorian era.

The fault lay in the mentality of that age. The groundwork in which the Victorian gardener placed his plants was prim, dull and lacked the one essential of successful gardening as we know it, imagination. Both inside and out gardeners followed each other like sheep; if one was successful with a new variety or species, it was quite certain to be grown by all the neighbours the following year. Garden design followed such stereotyped formulae that the formal Restoration gardens were imaginative beside them.

The bedding display was the main outdoor feature of the Victorian garden. In a few large estates it reached its greatest height, but even they could hardly compete with the acres of crude colours to be seen in great English gardens. The Victorian parterre of huge size with its beds kidney-shaped, or cut in lozenges, crescents, half-moons, diamonds and strange geometrical figures, was hardly so popular in the north. But parterres there were, usually of moderate size, cut out of the lawn or inside the walled kitchen garden. One of the largest was that at Drummond Castle where the old formal garden made an almost perfect site for a magnificent display of Victorian bedding. "The flower garden contains an area of nine acres tastefully laid out in the parterre style; the flower beds are tastefully diversified with many different varieties of colours and species; their respective heights and judicious arrangement of colours have been carefully attended, while the dazzling splendour produced by beds of scarlet Geranium, Verbenas, Calceolarias, and the choicest flowering annuals, presented a blaze of the greatest beauty imaginable. Spiral-shaped plants of Cypress, Holly, and Junipers &c, which are neatly trimmed and placed at respective distances, have a very imposing effect."[69] That gives an idea of the average Victorian gardener's standard of beauty.

It is a mistake, however, entirely to deprecate bedding displays. At its best it was a brilliant array of plants magnificently grown, although in our eyes its colour values may have been crude and the pigments were certainly laid on the canvas with a trowel instead of a brush.

Bedding in Scotland must have been seen at its best inside the walled garden, where the straight lines of walls, borders and paths tended to prevent the

formation of the grotesquely shaped beds of the
parterre. In most walled gardens bedding was confined to rectangular borders where the flowers were
planted so as to form their own pattern instead of
being intersected by innumerable paths. Two systems
of planting were popular: the ribbon, where long
rows were planted rising in height as they reached
the back of the border, and the panel, where various
designs were introduced by massed planting of
different varieties and colours. Standard Roses or
Fuchsias were often spaced at intervals so as to break
the horizontal plane. An example of this style of
bedding at The Hirsel in Berwickshire about 1870 is
shown in Fig. XVII. That bedding was so obviously
successful is only another proof of how adaptable the
walled garden was to various garden fashions.

In the middle of the century two gardens, both in
Midlothian, were particularly famous for their bedding displays, Dalkeith and Archerfield. A gardener
described what at the time was considered to be an
almost perfect display of bedding at Archerfield:
"The flower borders planted on the 'pannel system'
are intersected in two places by gravel paths, and
separated from the Vine borders by a broad gravel
walk running the whole length of the garden. The
centre division we considered best; it had for groundwork Mangles' Variegated Geranium; front row
Purple King Verbena, back row *Verbena venosa*,
backed up with white dwarf Dahlias, above which, in
bronzy waves, towered the graceful *Humea elegans*;
raised beds of Tom Thumb Geraniums, tipped with
immense specimens of Rollinson's Unique Geranium,

FIG. XVII.—VICTORIAN RIBBON BEDDING AT THE HIRSEL. FROM A CONTEMPORARY PHOTOGRAPH OF ABOUT 1870

towering 5 feet above the groundwork. Alternate
with these mounds are panels of Yellow Calceolarias
in circles, separated from the groundwork by a band
of Purple Verbena to give it weight as the visitor
passes along. The two end borders have blue Lobelia
for ground work, with mounds of scarlet Geraniums,
raised 4 feet above the groundwork; alternating with
the scarlet Geraniums are panels of Golden Chain
Geraniums; front row Cerastium; back row Alyssum,
backed up with Prince Arthur Dahlia and the beautiful Tritoma, time about."[69] The description is not
perfect, but it is quite clear that the contrasts of
colour left little to the imagination.

For examples of the ribbon border we can take
those at Wemyss Castle in Fife. Here in 1862 there
were two, 312 feet long and 7 feet wide. The back row
was formed of Sweet Peas in one border, in the other
Hollyhocks; the other rows were the same in both
borders. The second row consisted of Zelinda Dahlia,
the third *Calceolaria floribunda*, the fourth Geranium
Brilliant, while the edging was *Lobelia speciosa* raised
a little above the permanent Box edging, which was
universally grown throughout Scotland.[69] Ribbon
borders were popular in this garden; in another part
the back row consisted of Hollyhocks, the second of
Dahlia alba floribunda, the third of *Perilla nankin-
ensis*, the fourth of variegated Balm with an edging
again of *Lobelia speciosa*. In addition to a few beds of
which the dimensions are not given, the gardener had
to fill over 15,000 square feet with bedding plants
each year; and yet this was not considered a large or
an elaborate display.

127

Bedding plants had to pass a rigorous test of uniformity of growth and compactness of habit, so rigorous indeed that only a small number of varieties were commonly grown. Geraniums were naturally first favourites, of which there were about 30 usual varieties, including variegated forms. Other popular plants were Verbenas with 22 varieties, Calceolarias with 7, Pentstemons, *Salvia patens* and *S. fulgens*, dwarf Dahlias, Tom Thumb Nasturtium, *Cuphea platycentra*, *Cerastium tomentosum*, Heliotrope, *Humea elegans*, *Cineraria maritima*, *Lobelia speciosa* and variegated Alyssum, Ageratum, Balm and *Veronica speciosa*. Plants of loose habit, such as Petunia, were never seen in bedding displays.

On the other hand, small plants that formed neat edgings were in great demand. In the middle of the century *Lupinus nanus*, *Lobelia compacta*, *Saponaria calabrica*, Musk and the white Ivy-leaved Geranium were popular as edges for beds. In Appendix D will be found a list of annuals of 1855 suggested for situations other than bedding displays. It will be seen that it approaches nearer to our present-day lists.

Bedding displays took up so much time and labour that most other hardy herbaceous plants were ignored. Every now and then one finds in the horticultural press a lament that the old herbaceous border was sadly neglected: "I am one of those who think herbaceous plants much neglected owing to the rage for bedding out. I lament the extinction of the old herbaceous border or herbaceous collection, once a leading feature in most gardens of my

128

acquaintance".[69] A few large gardens still possessed herbaceous or mixed borders. There was a long one at Wemyss Castle, but visitors usually rushed past this without comment in their haste to rapturise over the resplendent colours of the massed annuals. The mixed border at Tyninghame must have been very fine, for it was one of the few that was regularly mentioned. But as a rule herbaceous plants were ignored; the relics of the old borders so loved by the previous generations were relegated to the edges of shrubberies where they gradually succumbed.

A few genera of hardy plants had a distinct vogue. Auriculas, among the oldest of popular flowers, were brought to a new pitch of perfection through the work of George Lightbody of Falkirk, one of the most famous names to be found in the history of the Auricula. The Pansy even excelled the Auricula and became almost a craze: this was particularly the case with owners of small and cottage gardens. One of the first men to improve the Pansy, which even to-day is one of the most popular flowers in Scotland, was a Mr Thompson of Iver, of whom little is known; but in the space of a very few years important nurserymen as well as local specialists were bringing out new varieties each year. Special Pansy societies were formed, and every flower show had several classes during the season. A Scottish Pansy Society was started in 1844; this held competitions in various towns in turn. The rules in 1854 for judging Pansies showed how meticulously the various points had to be examined:

1. The Pansy should be round, flat and very smooth at the edge.
2. Petals should be thick and of a rich velvety texture, standing out firm and flat without support.
3. Whatever may be the colour, the ground colour of the three lower petals should be the same.
4. Whatever the marks or darker pencillings they should be bright, dense, distinct and retain their character without running or mixing with the ground colour.
5. The two upper petals should be perfectly uniform. Two petals below must be alike and the marking in the eye and the three lower petals must not break through to the edge.
6. No flower should be under $1\frac{1}{2}$ inches across. In size there is a distinct point when coarseness does not accompany it.[69]

Another flower of lasting popularity was the Hollyhock. Classes for 18 different named varieties were not uncommon at flower shows. Although it grew extremely well in Scotland, the improvement of this flower was carried out in England, and the various strains of Baron, Parson, Chater, and Turner and Bragg each had their enthusiastic followers.

The chief claim to fame, however, of the Victorian gardener in England and Scotland was his skill in growing tropical plants, a skill which has never been bettered and rarely equalled. It is all the more remarkable if we realize that even after 1850 many of the greenhouses were old and still heated by means of hot-air flues. In 1862 a conservatory was still in use of the old type with a plastered roof and perpendicular windows which opened and shut by means of window cords; and yet in such a house the gardener was able to grow with great success such a difficult subject as *Ouvivandra fenestralis*, the Lace-Leaf Plant of Madagascar.

Almost every house of any size could boast of a conservatory. Many of those built during the first half of the century were treated architecturally as part of the house, with massive stone or wooden pilasters surmounted by a deep entablature and heavy guttering. It would be difficult to imagine more ungainly buildings, with a heavy roof, deep rafters and large astragals. The ventilation was inefficient, and the proportion of opaque to transparent was often higher than one to four.

As well as Cape Heaths, which were probably seen at their best at the close of the previous period, the most popular greenhouse genera were Camellia, Epacris, Alamanda, Leschenaultia, Pimelea, Eucharis, Gesnera, Bilbergia, and to a slightly lesser extent Orchids of various genera with Caladiums and Ferns as foliage plants, and *Primula sinensis* and Cinerarias for ordinary greenhouse decoration. *Oxalis cernua*, *O. caprina* and *O. rosea*, rare plants to-day, were often seen in greenhouses. Fuchsias were also grown in large quantities and in many varieties, but they had to have reflexed sepals and to be of contrasting colours. Selfs were considered worthless.

Winter flowering plants were not neglected. Among the most popular were Chrysanthemum, *Linum trigynum*, *Euphorbia Jacquiniflora*, *Gesnera zabrina*, *Poinsettia pulcherrima*, *Begonia fuchsioides*, *B. incarnata*, *B. manicata*, *B. nitida*, *Salvia splendens*, *Justicia purpurea*, *Hibiscus rosa-sinensis* and several forms of Camellia. Camellias were the most popular of all greenhouse shrubs. Some large gardens could boast of collections of over 100 varieties, but standard kinds numbered about 20. They were cultivated with great skill and care, with specimens over 15 feet high and the same in diameter not at all uncommon. One famous plant at Woodhall, a double white, was 18 feet in height and breadth, feathered to the ground. During the season the gardener was scolded if there were not more than a thousand flowers out at the same time.

The cult of greenhouse plants was not confined to great gardens. There were numbers of small enthusiasts in both country and town. A Dundee tradesman erected a small greenhouse on the few square feet available at the back of his house in which he was able to grow over 20 varieties of Camellia and other exotics in half the space at his disposal, while the other half was turned into an aviary.[66] There is also the example of the ambitious baker in Haddington who was so impressed by seeing the vinery at Yester that he made a kind of a greenhouse over his bakehouse oven where he succeeded year after year in growing most excellent grapes.[66] Then again there is recorded in 1852 the sale of the contents of a greenhouse belonging to Professor Dunbar of Edinburgh University, who apparently was not satisfied with small-sized plants. A *Rhododendron arboreum* fetched £5 15s.; a *Rhododendron cinnamomeum* was sold to the Royal Botanic Garden for £5 10s.; a double white Camellia, 16 feet high and 14 feet in diameter, fetched the "poor price" of £23 2s.; a *Camellia imbricata*, 14 feet high by 8 feet, £20; and a Deodar, 20 feet high, £6.[69]

Even more imposing was the amount of glass devoted to the cultivation of fruit. Almost all country houses of the mid-Victorian age could boast of at least one vinery and two other glasshouses with a row of Melon frames, while these increased in numbers to an almost incredible extent in great gardens.

Lord Ernest Hamilton described how at Drumlanrig in the time of the fifth Duke of Buccleuch "the piles and pyramids of fruit that crowded the dining room table at every meal were something altogether outside my experience. . . . I was told that no fruit which had once graced the dining room table should on any account make a second appearance there. Under this strange rule, huge bunches of grapes, with their symmetry hardly affected by the feeble assaults of those sitting near them, dived down into the lower regions after their debut, to be seen no more. It is clear that a system of prodigal consumption such as this could not do otherwise than make stupendous demands on the Buccleuch fruit supplies. These, however, never failed to prove equal to the demand. Langholm, Eildon and Bowhill could each boast large and prolific kitchen-gardens, but the main sources of supply were, of course, Drumlanrig and Dalkeith. The latter alone required a permanent staff of forty-two gardeners."

The range of houses at Blythswood, near Renfrew, form an excellent example of the lengths to which wealthy owners carried the indoor cultivation of plants. In 1862 the following houses were reported to be exceedingly well stocked:

1. Nectarine House, 36 feet long by 10 wide.
2. Peach House,   ditto.
3. Peach House,   ditto.
4. Vinery, 36 feet long by 14 wide.
5. Vinery for Black Hamburgs, 36 feet long by 17 wide.
6. Vinery for Muscats,   ditto.
7. Peach House, 36 feet long by 10 wide.
8. Apricot House,   ditto.
9. Apricot House,   ditto.
10. Fig House,   ditto.
11. Fig House, 50 feet long by 15 wide. There were also Orange trees and foliage plants in this house.
12. Orchid House, span-roofed, 40 feet long by 15 wide, filled with Cattleya, Phaius, Cypripedium, Lycastes, Dendrobium and Stanhopea.
13. Aquatic House, 32 feet long by 22 wide, filled with Dicksonia, Caladium, Cycas, Cyperus, Alsophila and others.
14. Ornamental Foliage House, 32 feet long by 12 wide, filled with such plants as Alocasia, Caladium, Erio-cnema and Cissus.
15. Flowering Plant House, 55 feet long by 30 wide, with many species of Cape Heath, Boronia, Acacia, and *Polygala grandis*.
16. Cucumber House, 32 feet long by 12 wide. This was used for propagating in the spring.
17. Melon Pits, 100 feet long.
18. Pineapple Pits, 100 feet long.[69]

The Pineapple was still grown in bulk until the end of the century, when the extensive importations from abroad made their greenhouse cultivation an unnecessary extravagance. Sometimes other tropical fruits were grown and ripened. One hears of the Guava, *Eugenia Jambos* or Rose Apple and the

Papaya, *Carica Papaya*; but the most outstanding was the Banana, which was of sufficient rarity in the '70's to warrant special dinners given in its honour when the fruit ripened.

With the excellent supply of indoor fruit gardeners and owners became more critical over the quality of hardy fruit. By the middle of the century most of the old Scottish varieties of Apples and Pears, which had satisfied previous generations, had disappeared. The number of recommended varieties had reached manageable proportions, and, indeed, differ little from those which are found in gardens to-day. For instance, in 1854 the following Pears were recommended for Scottish gardens:

Compte de Laney	Soldat Laboreur
Hessel	Beurre d'Amanlis
Louis Bonne of Jersey	Flemish Beauty
Bergamot d'Espères	Fondante d'Automne
Knight's Monarch	

All except Hessel, Soldat Laboreur and Flemish Beauty are grown to-day. The quality certainly improved to such a degree that on occasion Scottish gardeners could compete successfully in open competition. In 1852 the prize given by the Royal Horticultural Society for ten varieties of new Dessert Pears was won by the gardener at Duffus House, near Elgin.

Outside the walled kitchen garden Scottish gardens suffered severely from the Victorian lack of imagination. As time went on and manufactures increased the prosperity of Scottish towns, the big houses and gardens that appeared on their outskirts were just as hidebound in their mediocrity as any south of the border. They possessed the same banks of Bay and Laurel, or, as a sop to those who liked to see flowering shrubs, of *Rhododendron ponticum* or its hybrids, the same clumps of Laurustinus, Cupressus and Thuja, the same iron or rustic pergolas with climbing Roses, the same Ampelopsis or Ivy growing on the house walls, the same gravel paths winding amongst the everlasting Laurels, the same erection of glass refuse or white stones euphemistically called a rock garden, and above all the same Victorian villa parterre with its vulgar ostentation. The sameness of these glorified villa gardens can be dismissed; they did nothing to make gardening history.

In one branch of gardening Scottish gardeners did indeed make history: they were among the first to start the cultivation of alpines. Possibly this may have been due partly to the labours of the eccentric George Don: the memory of some of the lovely plants from our own hills which he cultivated in his Forfar garden may have inspired others. One would like to call him the Father of the Rock Garden, but there is no proof that his influence was so widespread, and there is a long gap between his time and the appearance of the first book written on the cultivation of alpine plants. This was *Alpines or Rock Plants*, by James Lothian, a rare little book, published in 1845.

Lothian was gardener to W. A. Campbell of Ormsary. Mrs Campbell was a keen gardener, and between them they made what was probably the first real rock garden in Scotland. Most of the plants were grown in pots and placed in position in the early spring after wintering in frames. The number of rare or difficult plants which they grew was quite remarkable: they included *Azalea procumbens*, *Cornus canadensis*, *Dryas Drummondii*, *Dielytra Cucullaria*, *Jeffersonia diphylla*, *Linnaea borealis*, *Primula altaica*, *Sanguinarea canadensis* and *Shortia galacifolia*.[43]

The idea of growing alpines must have been well received; within five years we find a suggestion for a garden with dry walls in which Sedum, Sempervivum, Saxifrage and Arenaria should be grown. In the summer show of 1854 of the Caledonian Horticultural Society were classes for alpines. The first prize went to Mr Smith of Melville Castle for *Dianthus alpinus*, *Phlox frondosa*, *Ramondia pyrenaica* and *Primula farinosa*, while second prize went to Mr Falconer of Canonmills Cottage, Edinburgh, for *Dianthus alpinus*, *Erigeron alpinus*, *Ramondia pyrenaica* and *Saponaria ocymoides*.

Shortly after 1850 Sir John and Lady Ord of Kilmorey went even further and laid out one of the first wild gardens. In a Birch wood on a hill slope with burns chattering down their gullies they made clearings among the bracken and planted ferns and alpine and bog plants. It must have been a fine garden, as it had the reputation of containing the best and largest collection of its kind outside the Royal Botanic Garden at Edinburgh, and Dalkeith.[69]

These pioneer efforts, however, counted for little. In the hands of the average Victorian gardener the rock garden deteriorated into a formless mass of slag among which a few plants of London Pride and Aubrietia lingered.

At the end of the previous period there were distinct signs that gardeners were beginning to realize the beauty of flowering trees and shrubs. Many of these exotics were American, and, even where the estate did not run to an "American" garden, Azaleas, Kalmias, Arbutus and Magnolias were quite common. Some gardeners in the west, and even in Fife, were experimenting with the hardiness of plants from New Holland, and one comes across a few references to *Eucalyptus Gunnii*, one or two Acacias and several Leptospermums making satisfactory progress in the open.[66] In the Victorian era this interest suddenly ceased. There are few, if any, references to shrubs in horticultural literature, and one may search the schedules of the various flower shows in vain for classes devoted to hardy flowering trees and shrubs.

The only stipulation about woody plants made by Victorian gardeners was that they must be evergreen. One cannot be so uncharitable as to believe them to have been quite insensible to beauty; and yet what excuse can we find in extenuation for planting thousands upon thousands of acres of their dull shrubberies? Perhaps they imagined that a dull background showed off the colours of their bedding plants; possibly their hands were so full with their houses and their annuals that they wanted plantations of something formed with the least labour; most probably the average flowering shrub did not fit in with their idea of beauty. It was an age of strong contrasts in colour, and the contrasts which they liked are not common in shrubs.

138

FIG. XVIII.—THE YEW ARBOUR AT KEIR

Whatever was the reason, the result was exceed-ingly dull. The remains of Victorian shrubberies are still to be found through the length and breadth of the country. There are estates where the process of elimination has been in progress for thirty years; and the end is not yet.

Plantations were usually made of Laurel and Bay, with Yew, Holly and *Rhododendron ponticum* as second favourites, and Ivy covering walls, banks and trees. Occasionally Lilacs, Philadelphus, *Viburnum opulus* and Laburnums were included, but in most cases they were soon smothered and only survived a few years. In that mock-heroic age Ivy was revered above most plants; a popular horticultural writer of the day summed up his love of the plant as follows: "The passing traveller sees, and pauses to enjoy the view—trees rising from beautiful carpets of Ivy on the sloping grounds, the Ivy ascending the trees as it lists, and waving in lengthened tresses over the brinks of precipices".[69]

To add enchantment to the scene various arbours and buildings occupied commanding positions. Over-topping a sea of Laurel would be a summer-house surrounded with a balustrade with stucco urns set at intervals. A clipped Yew pillar cunningly grown through its surrounding network of brick would occupy a central point.

Such sites differed in their treatment. At Keir there is a knoll at the end of a woodland glade where the Laurels have since been removed. The big trees remain and Rhododendrons and Japanese Maples take the place of the Laurels. On the knoll is a round

139

look-out house cunningly fashioned out of living Yews. Below is a half-moon-shaped bank smooth with closely shaven Yews, and at the bottom, in what is now a round bed of Azaleas, there used to be the family crest of the Stirlings made out of clipped Box. The Yew tower is probably much older, but the treatment of the surroundings was typical of the Victorian age at its best.

A Bridge of Allan Guidebook of about 1850 gives a description of Keir, typical of what visitors should look at in a good Victorian garden: "There is first the elegant fretwork of the massive colonnade, and the raised rockwork beyond; then the extensive conservatories, luxuriant in the richest plants, and teeming with the most delicious fruit: then groves of Coniferae, Pines, Cedars and Cypresses; banks of the Rhododendron, parterres of the Azalea, plots of the Geranium, and beds of Violets. Westward, the terraces become more spacious and still more varied, while vases of choice flowers and rustic erections add to their decoration". You will notice that the guidebook does not mention the acres of Laurel, which in this case must surely have been planted to act as a foil to the more brilliant colours and "rustic erections".

The one general exception to the dislike of flowering shrubs seems to have been Rhododendrons and, to a lesser extent, Azaleas. This was, of course, particularly noticeable in the west, where the larger species from the Himalayas grow particularly well; but in central Scotland and even occasionally on the east coast old hybrids, among them those of

R. arboreum and *R. barbatum*, the American *R. maximum* and the Himalayan *R. campanulatum*, were not uncommon. There are some fine old plants of *R. campanulatum* at Meikleour which must be at least seventy years old. Needless to say many were planted in shrubberies. Where they still survive they have been disentangled from the surrounding undergrowth, and so in many cases form poor specimens.

Among the early introductions of Rhododendrons to Scotland from the East were plants raised at Stonefield from seed sent home about 1835 by Dr. Campbell of Oronsay, who founded the Sanatorium at Darjeeling: these included *R. arboreum* and *R. campanulatum*.[51] But the greatest numbers of introductions in this period came through Sir Joseph Hooker. Many were sent home to his father, who at that time owned a small estate on Loch Fyne, and by whom they were distributed, particularly along the western seaboard. Many of the fine specimens of *R. Falconeri* and other Himalayan species which are to be found in western gardens were raised from seed sent home by Sir Joseph Hooker.

In addition, the value of named hybrids with their showy flowers was fairly generally realized. On a number of estates, although it was by no means universal, stands of hybrids were planted in the shrubberies, but the numbers were usually small, while Azaleas were grown in beds in parterres, almost the only shrub, other than Roses, to which such an honour was paid.

At The Hirsel, near Coldstream, there is a Rhododendron wood which must be unique in the British

Isles. Near the Tweed lies an area of many acres of rich, black, peaty soil. Several attempts had been made to plant this area with Spruce prior to 1860, but they always ended in failure. At last in desperation, and with admirable foresight, the Earl of Home decided to plant it with hybrid Rhododendrons and Azaleas. Planting went on steadily shortly after 1860, and again about 1890. Sufficient shade is provided by a few old Oak, Birch and Scots Pine. Below them the Rhododendrons have thriven amazingly, most of them being over 12 feet in height and of great spread. At the north end of the wood lies rising ground along which paths have been made. From these one can look down about the middle of June on a marvellous sea of colour, billowing to the far end of the wood. It is said that during the two planting periods every known hardy hybrid Rhododendron was included in this collection.

With such an example before them other landowners might have been tempted to follow the same plan with obvious advantage to their estates, but almost all were satisfied with the universal Bay and Laurel.

In no branch of horticulture did we follow England more closely than in the Rose garden. Paul's *Rose Annual* and Rivers' *The Rose Amateur's Guide* were scanned eagerly as soon as they came out. The large English Rose Shows were fully reported in our Scottish horticultural papers, and the Rose controversy of 1856 and 1857 between Paul and Rivers was keenly followed; arguments for and against the Manetti stock passed as briskly in Scotland as in

England. The only fact that comes out clearly is that we in Scotland grow Roses magnificently; several English observers remarked that the best Roses they had seen anywhere were in Aberdeenshire.

As with most other plants the Rose was not allowed to be natural. It was bedded and trained and tied in until it conformed to the ruling passion for excessive neatness. The usual form of Rose garden was oval with concentric beds and narrow intervening walks of grass or gravel. Pillars, wire baskets and chains on which were trained climbers were much in evidence. The Rose garden at Blythswood was typical: "The centre figure of the Rosary is a large oval, surmounted by a neat wire basket, and from it are festoons of wire for the support of climbing Roses; some very nice figures were cut in the grass, and planted with different kinds of Roses; the whole enclosed with a neat and handsome stone wall".[69]

Roses were used in much the same way as bedding plants. Ribbon borders, although not so common as beds, were not infrequent, while in both beds and borders flowering shoots were pegged down so as to give them as compact an appearance as a well-grown Geranium. Pillar Roses, usually formed of Perpetuals and Bourbons, were very popular, while standards began to come into fashion about 1860.

In 1860 three of the most popular bedding Roses in Scotland were Gloire de Dijon, Souvenir de Malmaison and General Jacqueminot. Most of the other varieties then grown have been entirely superseded.

While new greenhouse exotics were eagerly sought after, importations of new hardy plants from abroad were completely neglected. It is only rarely that one hears of any interest being taken in plant exploration abroad. The name of the great Robert Fortune was almost unknown in Scotland, although he was a native of Berwickshire. Occasionally half-hearted attempts were made to arouse gardeners' interest, but usually with complete lack of success. One such instance was a proposal of the Earl of Moray to send a collecting trip to Persia in 1855. To attract subscribers the subscription was placed as low as £1; but the enterprise never materialized.

There was one exception to this general neglect: Conifers were eagerly collected. Loudon states that the first Pinetum in Scotland was formed at Methven Castle, before 1830. A little later the big nursery firm of Lawson showed considerable enterprise in listing every exotic Conifer in cultivation. But what undoubtedly aroused the interest of Scottish landowners in ornamental Conifers was the introduction by Lobb in 1844 of *Araucaria araucana* (*imbricata*), the Monkey Puzzle, and of *Sequoia gigantea*, the Wellingtonia, by John D. Matthew in 1853. Accounts of these trees in the wild state and the germination of the seed sent home excited such tremendous interest that 5, 10 or even 15 guineas were gladly paid for young trees hardly out of the seed box.

The Monkey Puzzle was first introduced about 1795 by Menzies, but only a few seedlings were raised and none reached Scotland. By 1860 we are told that "As an ornamental tree the Araucaria is very generally used, and is much and justly admired in localities where it grows freely; it is to be found planted in

almost every villa; on the lawns and pleasure-grounds
of our nobility it is a great favourite. The sym-
metrical outline, the distinct and unusual appearance
of the tree, combined with the regularity and order,
which is observable in the beautiful arrangement of
its branches and foliage, causes it to harmonize well
with architectural erections, and to be frequently
planted in their vicinity; as a single plant on a lawn it
has few equals."[69] That was written by the head
gardener at Castle Kennedy and explains excellently
why the Monkey Puzzle was such a favourite in
Victorian days. The same gardener found, and was
able to propagate a variegated variety, which
delighted him beyond measure.

About the same time as Matthew sent home seed
of the Wellingtonia a portion of the bark of one of the
parent trees was shown at the Adelaide Gallery in
London. Afterwards for a number of years it was on
exhibition at the Crystal Palace in the north transept,
where "it dwarfed the gigantic Nubian Gods, which,
though of wonderful dimensions, are punies compared
to this tree". Its size excited the imagination of Scottish
foresters. Questions were eagerly asked in the press
each year about the rate of growth of the seedlings
and whether they were proving hardy. When everyone
found that it was totally unhurt by the frosts of 1860
and was of rapid growth when young, the demand
began. One of the reasons for the cost of this tree
was that importations of seed were few and far
between. After those of Matthew in 1853 and Lobb in
1855 a number of years passed before fresh supplies
of seed were obtained. The supply of young trees was

limited and everyone wanted it. A few avenues formed of it exist, but as a rule it was planted as a specimen tree on lawns or in the policy parks.

From 1840 to 1860 the formation of Pinetums was common in larger estates. In many cases so great was the interest that they were placed as close to the house as possible: for instance, at Methven Castle and Camperdown they began almost at the side of the house.

Many of the new introductions were collected by Scotsmen: Archibald Menzies, who first introduced the Monkey Puzzle, came from Aberfeldy; the great Douglas was born at Scone; Peter Lawson collected seed of *Pinus Cembra*; Robert Fortune, the first of the great botanical collectors in China, came from Duns in Berwickshire. Then there were two men who collected for Scottish syndicates: John Jeffrey, born at Lochore in Fife, who collected from 1851 to 1852 for the Oregon Committee of Scotland and who sent home seed of *Tsuga Mertensiana* (*Albertiana*) and *Abies Lowiana*; and William Murray, another Perthshire Scot, who was the first to send home seed of *Cupressus Lawsoniana* to Messrs Lawson of Edinburgh in 1854, along with further consignments of *Abies grandis*, *A. Lambertiana*, *Pseudotsuga Douglasii* and *Pinus ponderosa*. It is little wonder that our landowners became interested in Conifers.

It is remarkable what a number of Coniferae were collected in Pinetums in so short a period. In 1857 the following were growing at Craigo House near Montrose (modern names are given):

146

FIG. XIX.—ITALIAN CYPRESSES GROWING AGAINST THE HOUSE FRONT AT KEIR
PLANTED ABOUT 1845

Abies nobilis
    Nordmanniana
    Webbiana
    Pindrow
    sibirica
    Pinsapo
    cephalonica
Araucaria araucana (imbri-cata)
Cedrus Deodara
    atlantica
Cryptomeria japonica
Juniperus recurva
    chinensis
    excelsa
Larix europea
Libocedrus chilensis
    decurrens
Picea sitchensis
    orientalis
    Morinda

Picea jezoensis (this is four years earlier than the date of introduction usually given)
Pinus Cembra
    monticila
    excelsa
    Coulteri
    rigida
    mitis
    tuberculata
    ponderosa
    ponderosa var. *Jeffreyi*
    insignis
    sinensis
    Benthamiana
    Pinaster
    resinosa
    Laricio
    montana
Pseudotsuga Douglasii
Sequoia sempervirens

This was a very remarkable collection, of which many, particularly of the Pines, are now extremely rare in cultivation. Although Conifers are again being planted at Craigo, only about half a dozen trees of the original collection remain.

As the Victorian era advanced it becomes more and more impossible to differentiate between Scottish horticulture and that of other countries with a like love of flowers and the same kind of climate. Our gardeners were just as interested in the books of Dean Hole and the English gardening papers as those south of the Border: they were just as friendly or antagonistic to the efforts of William Robinson and Gertrude Jekyll to break away from the rut into which Victorian gardening had fallen: they were just as enthusiastic over the later introductions of the firm of Veitch and the new collecting stars rising in the firmament, Farrer, Forrest, Wilson.

It is said that history cannot be written correctly when the perspective is too close. Perhaps in the future someone may be able to find some differences between gardening in Scotland and gardening in England or New Zealand, differences due to some national trait and not to the exigencies of climate. At the moment it is beyond the powers of this author to do so.

CHAPTER VI

Botanic Gardens

FROM the earliest days the cultivation of plants and the science of medicine have been intimately connected. The Royal Botanic Garden at Edinburgh originated partly because there was no proper medical school in Edinburgh. One of the founders, Sir Robert Sibbald, was horrified at the exhibitions staged by quack doctors in Edinburgh shortly after the Restoration, where there were even performances on the tight-rope to attract trade if the supply of patients ran short. Almost 150 years later Dr. Jeffrey occupied the dual chair in Glasgow of Botany and Anatomy; in the morning he would occupy himself in dissecting a plant, and in the afternoon would operate on a body supplied by the public hangman.

While the primary idea of a botanic or physic garden was to supply plants for the teaching of medicine, it was not long before this was combined with the equally useful service of an experimental garden, to which new plants could be sent and where they could be tested, and from which they could be distributed, if they proved worthy.

The Botanic Garden in Edinburgh was founded in 1670 by Sibbald and others on a plot of ground in what was known as St. Ann's Yards at Holyrood. In 1676 the Town Council appointed James Sutherland as Intendant of the Physic Garden. It was from that date that its history really begins, for James Sutherland was a remarkable man and a very skilled gardener. A few years later he was made Professor of Botany, but unlike most botanists of his day he never lost his love of gardens. Within a short time he had brought together a collection of over a thousand plants and was always willing to distribute any surplus of the more ornamental species to his gardening friends and acquaintances. It was certainly owing to his generosity that many new plants were so rapidly distributed throughout our Scottish gardens. He travelled widely in Scotland, and had correspondents throughout Europe and the East and West Indies with whom he exchanged seeds and plants.

Soon the number of plants became far too large for the size of the garden; so in 1675 the Town Council handed over land near Trinity Hospital, at the east end of the Nor' Loch, near where the Waverley Station stands to-day, to which the collection was removed. The garden was only 300 feet by 190 feet, and was surrounded by a stone wall with a canal running through the middle of the garden. Sibbald described how "the walls also are covered with very beautiful shrubs. Roses of every kind are planted in beds at the side of the canal and also shrubs remarkable for their fragrant flowers."[26]

In 1683 Sutherland published a *Hortus Medicus Edinburgensis, or a Catalogue of all the Plants in the Physic Garden at Edinburgh,* In his preface he explained the reason for publication: "That I might thereby let the World know what Plants I could furnish to others, who are curious in this so useful a part of natural Philosophie, and what I could not; that so all who apply themselves to promote Natural History with me, might be encouraged to assist me in so good a designe, by making interchange of Plants, which they can spare and I want, with others which They want and I can spare".

In 1689 the garden suffered a serious set-back, for during the siege of the Castle it was thought necessary to drain the Nor' Loch, which completely inundated the garden and destroyed many of the plants. Sutherland petitioned for a grant to make good the damage, and in time the petition was granted.

In 1695 two further gardens were taken over as Physic Gardens, the College Garden and the King's Garden at Holyrood. Thus Sutherland was in charge of three gardens, all conducted as experimental gardens or for supplies of medicinal herbs.

Thomas Morer, a contemporary traveller, thought but little of the original garden: "On the north of the city in a bottom, is the physick-garden with 2700 sorts of plants, as the keeper of it told me. But then this variety of plants is all of its beauty, having no walks, and but little walling or good hedges to recommend it; and is (to my thinking) the rudest piece of ground I ever saw with that name. The manager of it, I suppose, guest my thoughts, and told me that he was taking a much more convenient field a little further off, which he designed to fence with a large brick wall, and, removing his plants thither, digest 'em into such a method as might make it a pleasant as well as useful garden."[52]

Nevertheless the gardens under Sutherland's wise and energetic rule gained a reputation that was almost European before many years had passed, a reputation which lasted until his death in 1719 at the age of eighty.

Then followed a period when they relapsed into gardens of little importance except for the supply of medicinal plants for students at the University. In 1789 the original gardens were abandoned and a new site was acquired near Haddington Place, off Leith Walk. This was laid out by Dr. John Hope, the Regius Keeper, still with the same arrangement of formal beds; but greenhouses were coming into fashion and those in the new gardens were of considerable size. The gardens were unfortunate in their principal gardeners; one or two promising young men died within a year or two of their appointment; others were unsatisfactory, among them George Don, who has been mentioned elsewhere.

Then came the great William McNab, who was appointed in 1810. Some description of his success as a gardener is given in Chapter X. On his appointment he found the garden, particularly the greenhouses, in a very bad state of repair. Much of the glass was broken and tropical plants were trying to survive their attempts to grow through the holes in the roof.

In 1823 the garden was again moved to its present situation at Inverleith. At the start a modest area of 14 acres was sufficient, which was increased in 1865 by the inclusion of the Experimental Garden of the Royal Caledonian Horticultural Society, which lay adjacent, and again in 1876 when the Town Council purchased another section of the Inverleith property and handed it over to the Crown to use as an Arboretum.

McNab accomplished the transplanting of the collections with consummate skill. The great Yew, still standing near the western end of the terrace, is known to have been moved twice, and, indeed, may originally have been planted by Sutherland himself.

From the end of the eighteenth century more and more plants were received from old students who collected abroad. Many were from the tropics and for many years the Botanic Garden was of the greatest interest and assistance to those who grew stove and greenhouse plants. Occasionally collectors, such as Menzies, sent home seed or plants from the more temperate zones, but it was not until Sir Isaac Bayley Balfour was appointed Regius Keeper in 1888 that there began that specialization in the flora of the Himalayas and the Far East for which the garden is now so renowned. The dividing wall between the Arboretum and the Botanic Garden was removed, the enormous rock garden was constructed, the herbaceous borders renovated and enlarged, the plant houses extended and work was commenced on the remarkable collections of Rhododendrons, Primulas, Gentians and other genera from the high hills of Asia.

The evolution of the Royal Botanic Garden into a place of beauty as well as of utility was largely the life-work of Sir Isaac Bayley Balfour, one of the few great botanists who have combined immense technical knowledge with a supreme love and admiration for the beauty of the growing plant. We Scottish gardeners have more to thank him for than we possibly realize.

The next botanic garden in size and importance is that at Glasgow. Before the end of the eighteenth century a small area of ground called the College Green, near the University, had been known as the Physic Garden, where a few plants were grown illustrative of botany.

About the beginning of last century there lived at Dalbeth, near Glasgow, a keen amateur botanist, Thomas Hopkirk. In the course of years he had collected together several thousand British plants. His enthusiasm was such that about 1816 he decided that Glasgow must have a botanic garden. He set to work and collected in a few months a sum of over £2000 from subscribers, who were incorporated as proprietors. He further made an agreement with the Faculty of the College of Glasgow to enter into a co-partnership agreement with them if they subscribed an additional £2000. Hopkirk also gave the new Society his entire collection of plants.[71]

Within a few months a site of 8 acres was purchased between the Dumbarton and Sandyford roads, and in 1817 the gardens were in being, complete with flower-beds, a rockery, a pond and several greenhouses. In *The Companion to the Glasgow Botanic Garden* there is a description of 94 of the most interesting plants which it contained. The first in the list,

Strelitzia reginae, was also the first plant to flower in the new gardens. As was to be expected at that period, much attention was paid to stove and greenhouse plants. Several Cactus are mentioned, such as the Night-flowering Cereus, also Palms, Passion Flowers, Hoyas, Agaves. The Telegraph Plant, *Desmodium gyrans*, caused a sensation, as it did at the Royal Botanic Garden at Edinburgh: "In our climate, the leaves in general only move during the middle of the day, and not in a regular manner, but with sudden jerks".[32] It is a peculiar list of plants, ranging from Strelitzia to the Mangel-wurzel.

By 1841 the original site was found to be too small, and the gardens were moved to their present situation in Kelvinside, which now consists of 47 acres.

Although the University had, and have, certain rights, the Glasgow Botanic Gardens have never been a University or Government institution. As so often happened, the committee had considerable difficulty in raising funds after the first flush of enthusiasm had passed; and in 1891 the Glasgow Botanic Gardens were taken over by the City. In its early days it was probably indebted to Sir William Hooker for its excellent collection of stove and greenhouse plants, for he occupied the Regius Chair of Botany at the University of Glasgow from 1820 to 1841. Since then it has always tended to specialize in tropical plants.

Up to the end of the Victorian era no other botanic garden in Scotland was of any interest or value to our gardeners.

CHAPTER VII

Seedsmen, Nurserymen and Market Gardeners

1

Seedsmen

As a rule catalogues of seedsmen and nurserymen are a help in gauging the popularity of various plants at the time they were issued. Unfortunately this does not help us much before the Victorian era owing to the common habit of listing large numbers of plants which were not actually grown in the particular nursery at the time, but which were in cultivation and might become popular in the future. Most of the old lists are also of little value owing to the lack of adequate descriptions; particularly is this the case with garden varieties, as, for instance, bulbs. Under the heading of Hyacinths, Blue, there might be a dozen or more names, but even such small differences as might have existed between the various blue Hyacinths were not described. Thus, unless the purchaser saw them growing his choice was largely a matter of luck: he was buying a pig in a poke.

Before the Reformation most of the supplies of nursery stock came from monastic orchards and gardens. Certain areas, such as Fife and Moray, benefited directly from the presence of nurseries

attached to monasteries where monks were sufficiently far-seeing to undertake propagation, particularly of fruit trees, on a fairly large scale.

Until the Restoration there was probably little
direct sale of plants or seed. The process of stocking
and restocking a garden was very different when
communications were incredibly bad, and when, in
addition, the garden flora was very small. Plant
breeding and selection were almost unknown. When
all seed was home saved there must have been a slow
but constant retrogression. The most that could be
hoped for was the exchange of seed among neighbours, and the slow dissemination of new blood when
plants or seeds were imported from England or the
Continent. In an impoverished land it was only
human nature to keep the best of the vegetables for
the pot and only to allow the poorest specimens to
set seed, with consequent deterioration in course of
time.

After the Restoration quality began to improve,
partly, no doubt, owing to the commencement of the
sale of seed and plants as a recognized trade. From
advertisements in the Edinburgh newspapers the
names and addresses of various nurserymen and
seedsmen can be learnt, but at the start their business
must have been small and the quality of what they
sold poor compared to London with its larger and
quicker turn-over. In 1683 we find two Scottish
dealers mentioned: Hugh Wood, "gardening at
Hamilton, dealing in fruit, seeds and numerous other
garden articles, whether English, Dutch or Scotch";
and Henry Ferguson, "seed merchant, at the Head

of Black Friars Wind", in Edinburgh. This was probably the same "Mr Harie ferguson" who is mentioned in *The Account Book of Sir John Foulis of Ravelston.* A collection of garden seeds was bought from him in 1689 which is interesting as showing the kinds of vegetables growing in Scottish gardens at that time:

4 unce Strasburg onion	.	16s. (Scots)
½ pund leiks . .	.	12s.
4 unce flanders onion .	.	12s.
2 unce beetrave .	.	8s.
2 unce parsneips	.	6s.
2 unce carets .	.	6s.
1½ unce turneip .	.	5s. 6d.
2 unce spinage .	.	5s.
1 unce cabage lettuce .	.	4s.
1 unce raddish .	.	3s.
2 drap marjorum	.	2s.
4 drap Indian cress	.	8s.
1 drap colliflour	.	7s.
1000 bowcaill plants	.	lib 2, 17s.
2 drap winter savorie .	.	2s. 2d.
1 unce scorzonera	.	14s.
260 cabage plants	.	lib 1, 0s. 6d.
2 pund turkie beans	.	10s.
3 drap silesia lettuce .	.	12s.
1 pund sugar peas	.	8s.
½ pund grein ransivall (Peas) .		5s. 6d.
½ unce yellow turneip .	.	2s. 6d.
4 drap selarie seed .	.	3s. [29]

It will be noted that Indian Cress is mentioned. This is the old name of *Nasturtium majus*. If Nicholson is correct in giving the date of introduction into England from Peru as 1686, three years is a short space of time to find it growing in a Scottish

FIG. XXI.—A VICTORIAN YEW PILLAR IN GOOD HEALTH

FIG. XX.—THE GROUNDWORK OF A VICTORIAN YEW PILLAR

garden. Until the beginning of the nineteenth century *Nasturtium majus* was always used as a vegetable or salad.

In this account-book flowers are rarely mentioned, but there are occasional entries, such as:

80 sets of Whyt Lily roots . lib 2		(Scots)
clowjuly flowers . . .	15s. 6d.	
75 tulip roots . . .	lib 1, 17s.	

There were other nurserymen and seedsmen, for we find Sir John Foulis buying "7 imps from Ye Gardener in Ye Surgeon's Yard, viz: a black pippin, a pear dangerous, 2 honie pears, a bon criteon, a swaneg, a bona magna plum", for which he paid lib. 4, 13s. 4d. Lady Grizel Baillie also bought seeds from Samuel Robson in Bridgend.

After 1700 notices of seedsmen became more common. In 1721 the following class of advertisement is to be found in the Edinburgh journals: "There is to be sold at John Weir's, gardener at Heriot's Hospital, and at James Weir's, son of the said John, his house at Tolcross, at the end of the West Port, all sorts of garden seeds, fruit and barren trees, and evergreens, as also flowers of the best kinds". Another well-known seedsman during the middle of the century was Patrick Drummond, "at his shop in the Lawn market, opposite to the Head of Libbertons Wind, Edinburgh". His catalogue of 1754 must have been one of the first to be printed in Scotland. It is bound in at the end of some copies of James Justice's *The Scots Gardener's Director*. As usual at that date no prices are mentioned. It is not of any particular interest, although it shows that gardeners were becoming more critical in the selection of their vegetable seeds and that varieties were becoming more numerous.

The preparation and quality of the seed left much to be desired. Purchasers were advised to rub Carrot seed between the hands; "For by the hairy substances with which their seed-vessels are covered, they adhere close to one another".[39] Justice complained that good Cauliflower seed was difficult to get both in Edinburgh and London, but that the best was obtainable from James Scot, a seedsman at Turnham Green. Seeds of some vegetables were regularly imported from abroad; for instance, early Beans were shipped every year from Lisbon.

In bulbs and flower seed by far the largest trade was with Holland, with firms well known in their day, such as Voorhelms Brothers and Van Zompel. Their catalogues were mere lists with names of varieties in each genus grouped under colour. Justice complained bitterly of the profusion of names and of the poverty of correct descriptions. He considered that it was entirely a matter of luck whether a purchaser chose a good variety or a poor one. The multiplicity of names was, indeed, astounding. In a catalogue of Voorhelms Brothers circulated in Scotland about 1756 there were listed 15 Fritillaries, 142 Hyacinths, 223 Tulips and no less than 120 Persian Ranunculus, besides a host of other bulbs and seeds. *Aster chinensis*, *Lilium pomponium* and *Lilium canadense* are also mentioned.

It is interesting to find that as long ago as 1754

Justice suggested that nurserymen should turn their attention to growing bulbs for re-sale to private gardens, a trade which even then was a monopoly of Holland. He drew attention to Leith as an excellent centre with a suitable climate and plenty of "Cow dung, sand, and of Tanners Bark, and of a dark, grey, sandy, Virgin Soil".[39] He also propagated many varieties of Hyacinth in his Edinburgh garden.

Apart from bulbs and an occasional specialized genus, like the Auricula, there was little selection attempted among perennials until the nineteenth century; but occasionally new varieties of annuals and biennials were brought out. Early in the eighteenth century one hears of "Pease, everlasting and sweet scented: Stockjulyflowers, white Brompton or red, Twickenham or purple, large Annual or ten weeks Stock, a curious late blooming stock; Wallflowers, yellow and bloody; Balsam, striped and female". This selection was done on the Continent or in England; in Scotland nothing was accomplished in this way until much later.

Towards the end of the eighteenth century planting had almost reached its zenith. A great demand for seedling trees of conifers and hardwoods sprang up, and before 1800 a number of important Scottish firms started of which several are in existence to-day. Owing to a steady demand for young trees they were able to expand in other directions. With very few exceptions they entered the general horticultural trade and sold seeds, bulbs and flowering plants.

2

Nurserymen

A few of the early seedsmen and nursery gardeners may have worked a small nursery in addition
to their general shop trade, but when gardening and
planting first showed signs of popularity most estates
ran their own nurseries. New introductions were
brought home by their owners by most haphazard
means. It has been stated that the parent Larches at
Dunkeld were brought in a handbag from London,
while the anti-Unionist, Lord Belhaven, brought one
of the first Cedars of Lebanon to be planted in
Scotland, in 1702, in a flower-pot tied on the top of
his baggage. This same tree by 1830 had reached a
height of 60 feet in the Beil garden.

Loudon states that the first two tree nurseries to
be established in Scotland were those of Malcolm at
the Water Gate and Gordon at Fountainbridge in
Edinburgh;[44] but no details are known.

One of the first nurseries to be established was
founded by John McAslan in 1717 on ground rented
from the Hutcheson Hospital in Glasgow, at the foot
of what is now known as Hutcheson Street. McAslan
was an important man, Treasurer of the City and for
thirty years Treasurer of the Buchanan Society. He
lived to a ripe old age. Robert Austin, who had
married his daughter, was made a partner in the
business in 1782; it was then styled McAslan &
Austin. To-day the firm of Austin & McAslan is
in the proud position of being the oldest established

nursery firm trading under the original name certainly in Scotland and possibly in the British Isles.

Robert Austin was one of the most energetic nurserymen in Scotland. In addition he had a thorough training. After serving his apprenticeship with Mr Glassford of Dougalston he went south, where he was employed at the nurseries of Grimmond at Chelsea and Hunt at Putney. On his return to Glasgow he at once started to produce the long series of seedlings of the Scots Rose for which the firm of McAslan & Austin were famous and which were so popular during the first half of the nineteenth century.

His correspondence with the brothers Aiton of Kew, with Sabine, the Secretary of the Royal Horticultural Society, and various nurserymen near London shows the great interest taken in these Scots Roses in the south. As they flowered, Austin sent collections of new varieties to the Garden of the Royal Horticultural Society, to Kew, and to the Royal Gardens at Windsor.

With the first consignment to W. T. Aiton, Curator at Kew, Austin wrote: "I have forwarded to your address per one of the Leith Smacks, a parcel containing two plants of each of the varieties of Scots Roses which I have had the good fortune to propagate from seeds. It is not to be understood that they all have equal merit, but many of them are very interesting. In our soil which is a light loam they require a mixture of sand and a quantity of well prepared cow dung. I presume that any part of Kew Exotic Garden with a mixture of loam and dung will produce them in great luxurience. The first year's bloom after transplanting is weak and often single, but you must not despond on that account, for as soon as they are established they improve in beauty and softness. When a group of them is in full bloom, they are as rich as a bed of Ranunculus, less formal indeed, but possessing more ease and elegance."

Austin's plan when negotiating with nurserymen was to send paintings of new varieties. Plants of those chosen were sold at 5s. 6d. per pair and were never retailed at less than 5s. each.

He showed refreshing modesty over his new varieties. In a letter to Sabine, dated December 31, 1819, he wrote: "I must in candour acknowledge that some do not display much striking variety of shade, yet still there existed such diversity of shape, size and general appearance, as I conceived justified me in separating them, but in this I will be most happy to be corrected by your superior judgement. It would require more fertility of genius than I possess to distinguish the whole of these varieties by appellations characteristic of their colours, habits, etc., which induced me to take licence of Florists, giving them the names of ladies, amateurs or encouragers of science, but will readily adopt such names as you think proper to give them."

Another early nursery was that founded by Robert Dickson in 1729 at Hassendeanburn in Teviotdale. He soon had a large and increasing trade; by 1753 his son, Archibald Dickson, was supplying trees to many of the big estates as far afield as Haddington and Midlothian. The firm's daybook for the period of

1753 to 1763 is still in existence. Although Dickson called himself a gardener, most of his trade was in forest and fruit trees. It is interesting to note the prices asked in 1753: Transplanted Firs (Scots Pine) 1s. a hundred, Laburnums 1d. each, Sycamores ½d., Limes 2d., Elms ½d., Apples 6d., Pears 8d., Plums 8d., Beech three a penny.

An average retail sale of ornamental trees for planting in the neighbourhood of house and garden consisted of:

24 Hollys for 7d.	12 Walnuts at 2d.
4 Silver Firs for 8d.	12 English Elms at 2½d.
6 Black Geans at 2d.	100 Crabs for 1s.

Together with 350 cabitch plants for 10½d, and 50 Wopen Cole for a penny.

His wholesale business consisted mostly of Whin seed, which must still have been uncommon as there are several entries of two or more pounds in weight. Seedling Scots Pine were also sold to other nurseries and seedsmen at 3s. per thousand, or four-year-old transplanted at 9s. per thousand.

This daybook is particularly interesting as containing a very early commercial transaction in Larch in Scotland. During 1753 a few were sold at 1½d. each; the next year they were sold in lots of 50 or 60 at a time.

Robert Dickson was the founder of a family famous in the Scottish nursery trade. In addition to Archibald Dickson who followed his father at Hassendeanburn, another son started the famous firm of Dicksons & Co., which is still flourishing with offices in Charlotte

Square in Edinburgh, while yet another son, James Dickson, founded in 1766 the Perth Nursery, afterwards called Dickson & Turnbull; this firm is now extinct, but in their day were most important.

By the end of the century Dicksons & Co. in Edinburgh were in the forefront of the nursery and seed trade. In 1794 was issued a "Catalogue of Hothouse, Green-house, Hardy and Herbaceous plants; flowering and evergreen plants, fruit and forest trees, alphabetically arranged". This is a curious publication as it was only a list: in the preface they stated: "We by no means pretend to be in possession of all the plants mentioned in this catalogue; perhaps no Botanic Garden in Europe can boast of such a treasure; notwithstanding, we are determined to increase our collection, and make it as complete as possible, to *supply* the demands of the public". As was usual at the time, no prices were given. It is difficult to see why such a list was published, unless it was as a feeler to see how much demand there was among the gardening public for new and rare plants.

Another catalogue of 1827 is much more interesting, both for the extraordinary number of plants listed and also for those named which are still considered as rarities, many of them American. Among the plants were:

46 Asters
28 varieties of *Chrysanthemum chinensis*
24 Dahlias
18 Delphiniums; all species except three with double flowers
24 Gentians, including *G. bavarica* and *G. verna*
34 Iris

21 Lilies; including *L. croceum*, *L. chalcedonicum* and *L. pomponium*
58 Narcissus; mostly species or forms of species
24 Phlox; mostly species
32 Primulas; including 7 of the old doubles
35 Saxifrages
31 Violas

Just as imposing are the lists of vegetables and fruit trees; of the latter 146 named varieties of Apples, and the same of Pears, are given, with no fewer than 194 Gooseberries; this was at the time of the Gooseberry craze.

Most interesting of all is the list of trees and shrubs: included among them are:

28 Maples
8 Arbutus; including *A. Andrachne*
41 Azaleas
Buddleia globosa
Epigaea repens
25 Heaths; all hardy and including *E. vagans*
Gordonia lasianthus and *G. Alatamaha*
Hydrangea quercifolia
10 Kalmias
All the American Magnolias, and, in addition, *M. conspicua*
Paeonia Moutan
Rhododendron arboreum
47 Salix
20 Viburnum; including *V. acerifolium* and *V. cassinoides*
487 Hybrid Roses

Dicksons & Co.'s nurseries at this time were in Leith Walk, Blandfield, Red Braes and Deanbank.

The Perth Nurseries specialized in forest trees, specially conifers, but they also accomplished much in other directions. They are said to be the original distributors of the double forms of the Scots Rose, *Rosa spinosissima*, and also of the Scarlet Hawthorn, *Crataegus oxycantha coccinea*. It was also one of the first firms to introduce the Swede Turnip into this country, as an envelope of seed was sent to them by Linnaeus.[38]

In 1796 we hear of them raising new Roses. Among them was one, at that time considered to be "perhaps the finest Rose yet produced in Britain". This was Venus, a small double white, thornless, with *Rosa alba* as the seed parent. Another well-known rose was Fair Maid, a semi-double pale red, in habit allied to Blush China. This had *Rosa centifolia* as a parent.[38]

It is difficult to-day to conceive the vast amount of planting which the great landed proprietors undertook between about 1775 and 1850. The greatest of all was the "Planting Duke", the fourth Duke of Atholl. Between 1774 and 1826 he planted 14,083,378 Larches and 13,348,222 trees of other kinds, a prodigious quantity.[38] To show how planting on this scale benefited the nursery trade it is only necessary to quote one instance; in 1824 the "Planting Duke" ordered from a Mr Urquhart, a Dundee nurseryman, 50,000 one-year-old transplanted Larch and 1,000,000 seedling Larch, of which one-half were to be delivered as seedlings, the other half-million were to be transplanted and supplied in the autumn of 1825.

This demand for trees stimulated the nursery trade to such an extent that it became a thriving profession. Nurseries sprang up throughout the country, some of them short-lived, others which exist to-day, although sometimes not under the same name. In 1826 there were three nurseries in Dundee, one of over 15 acres. In that year they distributed over $5\frac{1}{2}$ million young trees, while their output from 1817 to 1826 was over 45 million plants of all kinds, a large proportion of which were young forest trees. During the same period there were three nurseries in Brechin, only twenty-five miles away, which totalled 25 acres, a sign that the consumption in Angus and the Mearns was enormous. The same prolific production is to be found in other centres, such as Perth, Aberdeen and Inverness.

The largest of all the nursery firms was the Lawson Seed and Nursery Company of Edinburgh, which was founded in 1770 and was dissolved in 1884. The name still continues, but it was reconstituted later as a wholesale seed-house for farm and garden seeds. At the height of its success Lawson was certainly as large as, if not larger than, the great London firm of James Veitch & Son.

Like Dicksons & Co. they catered for every branch of the trade, from forest trees to bulbs and seeds. While they were not so enterprising as Veitch & Son in sending out collectors throughout the world, they occasionally bought seeds from collectors abroad. In 1855 they bought a collection of seeds from a Mr William Murray of San Francisco. This included *Pinus nobilis*, *P. Jeffreyi* and *P. Lambertiana*; *Abies Douglasii* var. *religiosa*; and *Cupressus Lawsoniana*; only 57 species in all, but including some most important introductions.

The firm, however, were more famous as propa-

gators, so much so that many young Belgian and
Dutch nurserymen used to come to Edinburgh for
training as apprentices. This training was intensive
and the work was very hard. Most of the nursery
work was done by apprentices with the exception of
weeding, for which old women from the Green
Market were paid 9s. a week. But it was not only in
manual labour that the apprentices were hard-worked.
At one period they were expected to recognize many
Apples and Pears by the appearance of the tree and
foliage alone. It was also not uncommon for them to
be able to pick out and name correctly thirty varieties
of Willow growing together in a bed.

The displenishing sale figures of Lawson's Windle-
strawlee Nursery at Granton Road on October 10 and
11, 1883, show the numbers of young forest trees
that were stocked even after the heyday of planting
was over:

Conifers:

Silver Fir	.	.	.	46,450
Larch 1-year	.	.	.	11,673,450
,, 2-year	.	.	.	1,372,100
Spruce 3-year	.	.	.	131,540
Scots Pine 2-year	.	.	.	1,474,400
,, ,, 3-year	.	.	.	465,500
Pinus cembra	.	.	.	15,560
Pinus Laricio	.	.	.	184,496
Austrian Pine	.	.	.	256,250

Hardwoods:

Lime	.	.	.	9,800
Horse Chestnut	.	.	.	15,900
Elm	.	.	.	106,290

Spanish Chestnut	.	.	140,100
Oak .	.	.	.	296,200
Ash .	.	.	.	101,600
Alder	.	.	.	1,649,200
Sycamore	.	.	.	330,780
Beech	.	.	.	1,172,900

Hedge Plants:

Thorn	.	.	.	412,000
Privet	.	.	.	188,400

Over 20,000,000 trees in all; and this was only from one of their nurseries.

Other important Edinburgh firms were Messrs Methven & Sons, and Messrs Cunningham & Fraser.

Towards the end of the century the trade in young forest trees began to dwindle at a very rapid rate and by 1900 was so small that stocks were being burnt. Many small firms went out of existence, while larger firms were reducing their acreage to suit the more modest requirements of stocks of garden plants.

Although John Forbes of Hawick did not start his nursery business until 1870, he held a most important place in Scottish horticulture in the later Victorian era, for he was one of the first men in the horticultural trade to realize that the hardy flower garden should not be confined entirely to bedding plants. Very early in his career he saw the great future for fine herbaceous borders, and specialized in Phloxes and Delphiniums among other herbaceous plants. Border Carnations and Stage and Alpine Auriculas were also favourites of his, while among greenhouse plants his

171

name will long be remembered as one of the first in the trade to take up the famous Begonia, Gloire de Lorraine, and as the raiser of its white counterpart which he called Caledonia. John Forbes always believed in the advantage of showing his plants as often as possible in flower shows throughout the country, a policy that has consistently borne fruit, for the firm, John Forbes (Hawick) Ltd., is one of the most important of those in the country specializing particularly in herbaceous plants.

Further north the nursery trade was in an equally flourishing condition throughout the nineteenth century. The first nursery of any importance in Dundee was owned by a Mr Urquhart, closely followed in size by that of a Mr Stewart; they were both great propagators of forest trees and sold them in enormous quantities during the first twenty-five years of the century. A little later, in 1833, W. P. Laird founded the well-known business afterwards called Messrs W. P. Laird & Sinclair, about the same time as his brother R. B. Laird started a similar concern in Edinburgh. For over a hundred years the family of Laird has been intimately connected with the seed and nursery trade in Dundee.

When the Stewart family gave up the nursery business about the middle of the century, part of their nurseries were taken over by the firm which ultimately became Messrs D. & W. Croll, Ltd. They also are well known throughout Scotland and further afield, specializing particularly in Roses and Potatoes.

Aberdeen has long been a centre of the nursery trade. One of the earliest firms was Messrs Benjamin

Reid & Company, who were established about 1830 as general nurserymen and seedsmen. Messrs W. Smith & Son, Ltd., on the other hand, who were founded in 1842 at Kintore close to Aberdeen, have specialized for almost a century in forest trees, of which they were and are one of the largest suppliers in the north.

Another well-known name in Aberdeen used to be Thomas Cocker. For many years he was famous as a Rose grower; indeed, it is believed that he served his apprenticeship with the famous William Paul. Cocker was a keen raiser of new varieties of several genera. Among Roses he introduced Mrs Andrew Carnegie, the scented Fra Carl Druski. The firm also produced some very fine forms of Trollius in shades which cannot be matched to-day; but Cocker's main claim to fame was in his strain of Bon Accord Double Primroses, such as Gem, Cerise, Purity, Beauty, Blue, Sulphur and Elegans. These charming plants are much sought for to-day. Even with our increased knowledge of plant-breeding, few modern varieties are so fine.

Finally some account must be given of that excellent botanist and eccentric individual, George Don. Born in the parish of Menmuir in Angus in 1764, he was brought up to the trade of clockmaker, but at an early age his love of plant-collecting made the mending of clocks not only irksome but quite impossible owing to his many long absences searching the hills for plants.

He then turned to gardening. He was certainly employed at Dupplin Castle and probably at Hewell Hall in Worcestershire before returning to Forfar in

1797, where he started a nursery at Dovehillock on ground sloping down to Forfar Loch. This was his home until his death in 1814, except for a short period of three years from the end of 1802, when he was employed as head gardener at the Royal Botanic Garden at Edinburgh. This appointment was not a success: he was certainly a better botanist than the Professor, but he was a very poor gardener and was completely ignorant of greenhouse plants and their management.

It is impossible to improve on Dr. Neill's account of Don's nursery which appeared in the *Scots Magazine* of June 1809:

"The existence of a flower garden and flower nurseries at Forfar, which for number, diversity and rarity of the hardy plants cultivated in it are perhaps scarcely to be surpassed in Britain, is a fact not generally known. We think it right to give it what publicity is in our power, both as a piece of interesting information to botanical amateurs, and of justice to the indefatigable exertions of Mr George Don, who, we understand, has surmounted many difficulties in following out his favourite pursuit, and in forming so extensive and curious a collection of living plants. The whole of the plants are of a hardy sort, Mr Don not possessing either green-house or stove for the protection for such as are tender. It is in alpine plants and in hardy perennials, and annuals, that the Forfar garden excels. The garden is situated on a bank which slopes down to the lake of Forfar, not far from the town; and it fortunately includes a great variety of soils, from dry to peat bog. No place could be found more favourable for alpines and aquatics, which are in general found to be of rather difficult cultivation, but which flourish here as in their native habitats. . . . To give some idea of the extent of the collection, I shall mention the number of species of several genera which are at present growing in the garden. Of the genus *Veronica* there are 55 species, of *Salvia* 50 species, *Campanula* 44, *Allium* 40, *Saxifraga* 46—some of the rarest ones, as *S. Coesia*, *S. Petroea*, *S. rivularis*, etc.; *Dianthus* about 20 species, *Cucubalis* 13—being the whole ever cultivated in Britain; *Silene* nearly 50, *Fumaria* 14, the genera *Ononis*, *Lathyrus*, *Vicia* almost complete, *Astragalus* 40 species, *Trifolium*, no fewer than 69, *Hieracium* 44. It were needless to enumerate more. The botanist will form a due estimate of this collection on being told that he may see here upwards of 60 species of *Carex*, flourishing in great perfection. The agriculturalist may here find the whole of the hardy *Gramina* carefully distinguished and arranged, amounting to over 100 kinds. This season Mr Don has introduced several hundred species of hardy plants, most of which we are told have never before been cultivated in Scotland.

"The Forfar garden, it must, however, in conclusion be confessed, makes very little external show, being in a great measure destitute of the ornament which arises from neat alleys with hedges or edgings, or well laid-out or well-kept gravel walks. It is, in fact, merely an uncommonly excellent collection of hardy plants; and while it would doubtless fail to please the lover of tasteful gardening, it would as certainly prove highly interesting to the botanist and to the curious cultivator. Mr Don, we have been told, has an ample nursery of rare hardy plants, for which he receives orders from the curious in different parts of Britain; and when the proceeds of these shall enable him, we understand it to be his intention to improve the exterior appearance of his garden.''[67]

Most of the plants were grown in a long border in botanical arrangement, apparently almost all un-labelled. It says a great deal for his knowledge that he made so few mistakes, but during his long absences in the hills affairs were in a hopeless muddle. In addition he grew some trees to help to supply local needs.

It is not surprising that such a nursery was a financial failure. The only possible customers were botanical institutions and private botanists rather than gardeners. Towards the end of his life he was in a constant state of penury.

This eccentric genius did nothing for gardening plants; he never wrote except on systematic botany; he never showed any real love of gardens; and yet it is possible that indirectly he did a great deal towards preparing the way for rock gardens and the cultivation of alpines.

3

Market Gardeners

Little is known of the early days of market gardens in Scotland. Probably there is nothing much to learn, because market gardening as a trade was bound to languish at a time when vegetables entered little into the diet of the nation. One comes across a few seventeenth-century references which show that one or two market gardens existed near Edinburgh before the Restoration, or at least that there were some gardeners who were in the habit of selling their surplus. For instance, Monktonhall is quoted as an old garden which about 1630 was accustomed to supply fruit and vegetables to Dalkeith.

After the Restoration the practice became commoner. We hear of a portion of the garden at Holyrood being let to a William Miller, who grew produce for market and also sold seeds. In 1702 Dalkeith was again supplied, this time by John Arro, who must have owned a nearby market garden. A little later, after the Rebellion of 1715, a number of gardens belonging to forfeited estates were let by the York Building Company to market gardeners, among them that of Winton House.

In 1742 we find an example of the practice, so common to-day, of letting the kitchen garden to a professional gardener in return for a small rent and a supply of vegetables.

To WILLIAM DODS, Gardner at Wauchton

I hereby offer you my gardens commonly called the Kitchen as likewise that called the Priest yard from the date herof to the term of Martinmass next, for nine pounds sterling of Rent payable at Lammass and Martinmass next by equal portions; you likewise furnishing my house with all kind of kitchen garden stuff (fruit excepted). . . .

JOHN HALL

In the eighteenth century market gardens were called Mail gardens, as their produce was carried to

Edinburgh or Glasgow. The first large market gardener to supply Edinburgh was a man called Henry Prentice, who cultivated Peas, Turnips and Potatoes on an extensive scale about 1746. Before that date supplies were carried to market in baskets, and his was the first market-garden cart to appear on the streets. By 1771 the acreage of market gardens near Edinburgh was about 125, which by 1812 had increased to 400, but this included bush fruit. The supplies must have been more than sufficient. William Creech in his *Edinburgh Fugitive Pieces* recounts how in 1781 Admiral Parker's fleet and a Jamaica fleet, together with several hundred merchantmen, lay in Leith roads for seven weeks. The crews were suffering from scurvy and fresh vegetables were supplied daily as antiscorbutics to many thousand men; yet so plentiful was the supply that the local prices were not raised at all.

The average annual consumption in Edinburgh about 1810 of bush fruit was about 50,000 Scots pints of Gooseberries, 15,000 of Red Currants, 15,000 of White Currants, 2000 of Black Currants and only 1000 of Raspberries. By the end of the eighteenth century the popularity of Strawberries had increased, and between 60,000 and 80,000 Scots pints were sold in Edinburgh each season.

A similar increase in market gardens and orchards is to be found near all the larger towns. Dundee had the reputation of being particularly favoured in its supply of vegetables, for market gardens were plentiful and prices unusually moderate. Between Lanark and Hamilton there were about 220 acres under fruit by the year 1810, of which the crop sold for about £3400 in 1812. Other excellent areas for fruit were the Carse of Gowrie and Tweedside: in fact the latter exported a fair quantity of fruit each year to the North of England. As early as 1765 the Newcastle carrier employed five horses during the season carrying White Warden Pears from Jedburgh to Newcastle.

CHAPTER VIII

1

Cottage Gardens

THE picture of an old Scottish hamlet is most depressing. As late as the middle of the eighteenth century in parts of the country off the beaten track it was rarely more than a group of huts made of mud and turves clustered together for shelter, often lying in a depression with undrained and sour soil. The roofs were so low that it was difficult for a full-grown person to stand upright. There were no windows except an occasional unglazed hole in the wall, while the chimney was an opening in the roof. This abode was shared by the family, the fowls and the cow. The interior reeked with moisture and was very filthy.

It is not surprising that the surroundings were equally uninviting, a quagmire in winter and a noisome dust-heap during a summer drought. Close to the huts were the middens with the kailyard along-side. Here was grown the universal Kail which for many centuries formed, together with oatmeal, the most important articles of diet of the poorer classes of lowland Scots.

Of cultivation, as we know it, there was none. The soil was never drained, or manured unless it lay below the midden, when the scourings ran into it. In the middle of the eighteenth century the only improvement was the digging-in of the old turves from the roof. The surface of the soil alone was scratched, as trenching was never practised. Seed was home-saved and always came from the poorest plants. Everything was planted too close, with the consequence that production was lowered instead of increased.

This unfortunate picture was due to several causes, of which the chief was the bad system of yearly tenancies; another was the extreme conservatism that was universal in country districts. It is often stated that the poorer classes in lowland Scotland were better educated than their equals in England owing to the system of parochial schools. That may be so; but it is also true that after the Reformation schoolmasters and clergymen were as pig-headed and ignorant about practical matters of agriculture and horticulture as their charges. It is a curious fact that there have been few outstanding gardeners in Scotland among clergymen or schoolmasters.

Improved methods and ideas were absorbed very slowly; what was good enough for the previous generation was always good enough for the present, at any rate until 1750. For that state of affairs the parish ministers and school teachers must take their share of blame. Many of them were kindly and thoughtful about the well-being of their flock, but they rarely tried to improve the productivity of the land. Perhaps it could not be otherwise. It is difficult for us to-day to visualize the watertight compartments into which most of rural Scotland was confined owing to lack of communications. If a minister travelled at all, it was only to preach in a neighbouring parish or possibly once a year to attend the Synod in Edinburgh, a laborious journey on horseback. Where the parish minister and school teacher would not lead the way, there was little incentive for the poorer classes to improve their land and crops.

Before the middle of the eighteenth century the usual diet was Kail brose and Kail soup; the former was made of Kail shredded and boiled and then mixed hot with oatmeal; the soup was a sodden mass of Kail and water, occasionally with an old hen boiled with it. Even in summer the outside leaves of the young Kail were picked off and made into soup; these leaves were called Stowans. If there was room in the kailyard, Bere was grown for pot Barley, which was used, so long as it lasted, as an additional ingredient in the soup. The only other vegetables grown were Peas, Beans and more rarely Turnips with Parsnips at a later date.

Parish ministers and teachers were almost as poor and were satisfied with the same diet. Meat was rarely seen, but in coastal districts fish, usually salted, was eaten by all classes. In towns the diet was much the same. Up to the end of the seventeenth century most town houses, even tenements, had their own kailyards. It was not until the standard of living improved considerably that market gardening on the outskirts of towns became a staple industry.

Great gardens, where improved cultivation was practised and the importance of a plentiful supply of vegetables was realized, certainly acted as centres from which a better understanding of gardening sprung. "Improving" landlords, such as John Cockburn of Ormiston, by precept and teaching must have done a great deal, but records show that the change for the better was slow, far slower than it would have been if the people had been less conservative. Several gardeners were allowed to give away surplus seed and plants to nearby cottagers, but one does not hear of much real improvement until after 1750, when the countryside suddenly began to realize the value of good tillage.

Highlanders were even more backward; indeed, until after the '45 they did not include vegetables in their diet and actively disliked them. The Clan Grant were among the first to cultivate kitchen gardens, and for many years were called "the soft kail-eating Grants".[42] A century later the usual vegetables cultivated in the highlands were Kail, Cabbages, Onions, Carrots, Beans, Peas and Potatoes.

From the middle of the eighteenth century advance in cottage gardens was rapid and moved equally with the improvement in agriculture. It might have been even faster if security of tenure had been more certain. By the end of the century there were four classes of cottage gardens: (1) Those held in feu. (2) Those held on a yearly tenancy. (3) Gardens of farm servants. (4) Village gardens.[54]

Apart from usually being the largest, a garden held in feu was also the most likely to be the best cultivated owing to security of tenure. Villages were certainly cleaner, with better built houses and a consequent improvement in their gardens, but those held on a yearly tenancy and the gardens of farm servants saw little change until the nineteenth century when their general conditions were bettered.

In gardens held in feu, in addition to the usual vegetables there was often a row of Gooseberry bushes, a few red and white Currants and an Apple or Pear tree next the house. Where cottage gardens were of some size Wheat and Flax were grown as regular rotation crops.

There was a notable increase in the variety of vegetables, but the great new garden crop was the Potato. This was now a staple article of diet. In 1812 it was reckoned that a family of six consumed 2688 pounds of Potatoes per annum. So much was it appreciated that it was the custom in country districts, where few cottage gardens exceeded an eighth of an acre, for the cottagers to apply to a nearby farmer for a ridge in a field so as to increase the Potato crop.

Unfortunately the quality and quantity of the garden produce was still poor owing to the persistent habit of collecting home-saved seed. For many years the cottagers on the braes of the Carse of Gowrie had found a ready market in Perth for Kail seed, which ripened well on the slopes of the Sidlaws. This must have meant a considerable increase to the income, as it sold for 2s. a pound wholesale. But complaints about the quality became more frequent when it was found that in most cases Cabbage, Savoy and Kail were grown next each other in the same plot.

Manure was still scarce, although pigs were more often kept, partly for manure and partly to eke out the winter supply of meat. They were killed in the autumn and salted.

For many generations a few herbs had been grown in cottage gardens. A great favourite was Elecampane, which was considered to be a general panacea for all ills. Rue was used for ulcers, while Tansy was believed to be a sovereign remedy for worms in children. Two other common herbs were Horehound and Camomile.

Some flowers were now to be seen. By far the most popular was the common Marigold, which was allowed to take control of some corner. So much of a pest did this become in some districts even before the nineteenth century that a clause was sometimes inserted in the lease fining cottagers who allowed it to get out of control. Polyanthus, called Spinks in the lowlands, were also popular, and so were Wallflowers, London Pride, Thyme, Spearmint and Southernwood. The only common Rose was the Red Cabbage.

In some towns artisans' gardens were on a higher level of cultivation, as is instanced by the famous Paisley Florists' Society which is described in Chapter IX; but, excepting on rare occasions, little was done to encourage the artisan to grow anything except vegetables. We have to wait until 1852 before classes for working men were started at the Glasgow Horticultural Fair; these included 3 plants in pots, the best 4 Pansies and 4 different Gooseberries.[69]

Even in the middle of the nineteenth century complaints were still heard from country districts about the poverty of cottage gardens. Many were still undrained and the only manure was old turves or thatch off the roofs. The cottagers had little idea of good cultivation; digging was skimped and was rarely completed before April. In order to combat the age-long inertia a start was made to form cottage garden societies. Among the first were those of Kincardine and Kilmadock which did much useful work in encouraging a competitive spirit. Certain districts began to specialize in one particular plant; for instance, the popularity of the Leek in Ayrshire was unbounded. Local competitions were held and the size of some of the winning plants was enormous. These societies have been of the greatest assistance in fostering the spirit of gardening. There are very few areas where the classes at the village flower shows are not eagerly contested. After centuries of neglect the cottage garden in Scotland has certainly come into its own.

2

Farm Gardens

As farms increased in acreage and longer leases were granted, it is only natural that farm gardens increased in size. Here, however, we have to note a curious anomaly in the exact definition of the term garden. Lord Kames gave an excellent example of this difficulty of definition. In his day farm gardens often supplied food for stock as well as vegetables for the family. To show to what a length this was carried we only have to read: "Where red clover is one of the crops (on the farm) in the rotation, a kitchen-garden need not exceed two or three acres. Where red clover enters not into the rotation, six acres are the smallest quantity even for a single plough; because it must yield food for man and beast. Two acres are necessary for summer food to cattle; two more will be usefully employed in cabbage, colewort, turnip, carrot, potatoes, leeks, onions, Turkey-beans, white peas, and other kitchen stuff for the family. The remaining two acres must be sown with barley and red clover."[37]

This mingling of farm and garden produce in the so-called kitchen garden was not of great age. Prior to the eighteenth century farm stock had to forage for itself.

White Turnips were grown in a few gardens in the early seventeenth century, but Swedes did not appear until well on in the eighteenth. Hay was almost unknown, and Potatoes, as has been explained before, were an expensive luxury until about 1775.

It was not until the end of the eighteenth century that fodder for stock began to be field grown and farm gardens dwindled in size. Fruit was still rarely seen, and was confined to an occasional Apple or Pear tree and Gooseberries and Currants. Flowers were even scarcer.

Like cottage gardens, farm gardens began to improve early in the nineteenth century, but those of good quality were sufficiently rare to have special note made of exceptional examples. A Mr Hunter of Blackness drew attention in 1811 to a very fine garden at Keppoch on the river Spean:

"I was conducted to the garden, which I found situated on a sort of bank, sloping towards the river, surrounded by an old thorn-hedge, and sheltered by a few spruce and larch firs of a good size, and in a very thriving condition, of the age of about 35 years, as I guessed. I particularly noticed that this garden was not even their best soil, there being a haugh of fine land beyond it, towards the river, in which were their drilled crops, turnips, potatoes, and some corn.

"On entering this garden (or rather orchard), the loads of apples and pears, and the vast size and healthy appearance of the fruit-trees, absolutely astonished me:—in fact, I think I can venture to assert, that I have no recollection of ever having seen a greater crop on the same number of trees, in any one place. As I have said, the trees were of a very large size in general, and they were loaded with fruit, from the lowest to the top branches, which last were bent quite downwards in a pendulous state. Many of the younger and smaller trees were propped and supported by forked sticks; and other branches were shown to me, which had been broken down by the weight of the fruit. . . . I observed of apples, the White Hawthorndean, Strawberry, and Redstreak, and an apple generally called the Sugar and Water; and of pears, the Early Carnock in great abundance, and of excellent colour and quality; and the uncommon little excellent pear called John Monteith's; the fruit of this last, very small and much scabbed, but of good flavour. I perceived they had the Crawford or Lammas, but its fruit was past. I looked in vain for our excellent Scots pear, the Achan; it did not seem to exist in the garden.

"Great as was my surprise with the apples and

188

pears, it was nothing when compared with that excited by the plums. There were several trees loaded to excess with the true Damson (if I be not very much mistaken, but which I am unwilling positively to assert it was;) in fact the trees were clustered with them, and literally *black and blue*, as was the ground below them: For this fruit seemed to be utterly disregarded, not being a good eating plum. I recommended strongly to Mr M. to order a stock of sugar, and preserve them in pots; when he could not fail to turn them to excellent account.

"I next took particular notice of a good-sized roundish pale-red plum, somewhat resembling the Imperial, though assuredly not it; and even a better fruit, as I thought. With this plum I confess myself unacquainted; the stone was free, in a large open cavity: the flesh and flavour extremely good.

"But I am well acquainted with the two next I have to mention, the Yellow Magnum and Greengage, both thriving luxuriantly, and with excellent crops of fruit; the Magnums large, well-shaped, free from gum, and of a rich yellow colour all over; the Gages, of the true brownish and green colour, and completely ripened, though some of them were cracked by the rains. These were growing on standards, in the heart of Lochaber, and where the snow on the tops of the hills was visible to us from the garden on the 23*rd of September*! And so little were they thought of, that our conductor did not know their names, in English at least, and I did not enquire whether he did so in Gaelic. Indeed he took more delight in calling our attention to a stock of shot

cauliflower, as being a much finer thing: more uncommon in that garden it undoubtedly was, being at
the time quite unique.''[10]

Such farm gardens are almost as uncommon to-day.
It is rarely that one meets a keen farmer-gardener;
perhaps they have to live so close to the soil that
they cannot bear the idea of delving again into the
earth in their spare time.

3

Villa Gardens

From their commencement the gardens of villas
seemed to have produced more than their fair share
of criticism. The term villa garden seems to have
been loosely used. In the eighteenth century, at any
rate, any small house with a garden of not more than
an acre was often called a villa. As the popularity of
horticulture increased, their owners were puzzled
how to lay out a small garden, and in desperation
were forced to copy large gardens in the neighbourhood. This brought down on their unfortunate heads
the pungent scorn of the doughty Lord Kames, who
wrote: ''The citizen, who in his villa has but an acre
for a garden, must have it diversified with every
object that is suited to an extensive garden. There
must be woods, streams, lawns, statues, and temples
to every goddess as well as to Cloacina.'' He called
this ''raising a jumble of emotions''.[36]

Later, in 1823, when villa gardens were sufficiently
numerous to have a book written for their sole

benefit, the author, Walter Nicol, complained that they tried to ape "Places". He disliked the belt of trees so commonly planted round the smallest garden, and the ostentation of two gates where one would have done. Unfortunately Nicol wrote a dull book, full of useful cultural hints, but he fought shy of grappling with the subject of the design of small gardens.[56]

The Victorian gardening press was also uniformly critical, but it was usually destructive and not constructive. One author suggested, in 1852, that mixed borders were the most suitable forms of planting. He advocated dwarf evergreens, *Polygala chamaebuxus*, dwarf Rhododendrons, double Wallflower, Helianthemums and Butchers' Broom in the front row; Mahonia, Aucuba, Sweet Bay, *Garrya eliptica*, Laurustinus and Rhododendrons in the second row; Laurels, Bays, Yew and Holly in the third row, planted six feet apart and backed with a row of Spruce.[69] This was a curious and ugly mixture.

Whatever criticisms may be laid at the Victorian type of gardening it was certainly not suitable to small gardens. With few exceptions the villa garden in Scotland was carried on in an incredibly dreary form until a few years ago. One of the chief causes of complaint, which can be carried back to Victorian days, was the existence of large trees and overgrown bushes in an area that was far too small for them, a state of affairs that is still far too common.

CHAPTER IX

Horticultural Societies and Flower Shows

COMPETITION in moderation has always been a strong incentive to gardening. Scottish gardeners have long been aware of this, and horticultural societies with their accompanying flower shows have taken an important place in our gardening life for over a hundred years. Indeed, if the difference in population is taken into account, we realized the importance of local societies and local flower shows far earlier than did English gardeners. In a way, no doubt, these local societies were direct descendants of the various "improving" societies which were formed in various localities to teach farmers how their land could produce better crops. Horticultural societies have never limited their activities to flower shows alone; in almost every case from their commencement they held winter meetings for lectures and discussions, meetings which were, and are, very well attended.

Pride of place must undoubtedly be given to the Paisley Florists' Society which was founded in 1782. At the end of the eighteenth century Paisley was quite remarkable for the intelligence of its inhabitants. They took great pride in their houses, were members of the many reading societies which flourished there, while the operatives were noted for their pigeons and bees which they kept in large numbers.[9]

Some of the rules of this Paisley society were peculiar. Eight flowers were called Competition Flowers, Auricula, Polyanthus, Hyacinth, Tulip, Anemone, Ranunculus, Pink and Carnation. All others were classed as Border Flowers, although they also could be shown. Of Competition Flowers by far the most popular was the Pink. It appears that a supply of fresh seed was obtained from London about 1785. Among the resultant seedlings were some laced varieties which had never been seen in the district before. After that a craze for the Pink began which lasted for generations, and in time the members evolved their own particular type of flower. In their eyes the quality of the lacing was everything, but laced flowers should not have fimbriated petals. White body colour was essential, and then in order of esteem came black lacing shaded with red towards the centre, scarlet and purple lacings. Doubles were popular but were not imperative for the show bench.

Every year from 40 to 100 manufacturers, tradesmen and artisans (it was a very democratic society) met for dinner and for showing the particular Competition flower selected for that year. Each of the eight had their turn, but the Pink was shown twice as often as any other flower. The first prize was a silver medal, suitably inscribed, worth about a guinea. It was awarded to "The person who presents, of his own rearing, the twelve specimens of the competing flower which taken collectively are the best".

The second prize was another silver medal worth 15s. After the awards the flower for the next annual competition was announced.[9]

As an example the competition was held on June 5, 1830, that year for the twelve best Tulips. The first prize was awarded to William Adam, weaver, Caledonia Street; the second to James Adam, weaver, Caledonia Street; the third to William Robin, weaver, North Street; and the fourth to John Wylie, weaver, Ferguslie.

In addition to the main competition there were meetings every Thursday evening from the time of the flowering of the Polyanthus to the disappearance of the Carnation in late summer. At these meetings every member had the right to show specimens of as many of the Competition Flowers as were in season. The Prize was the enrolment of his name in the minute-book. Border flowers were also shown, but in this case the prizewinner's name was entered in an inferior book called "The Competition of All Flowers Book". At the end of the year totals were counted up and the most successful competitor received a spade, the next a rake, and the third a trowel or knife.

The fact that the society still exists proves the keenness of its members through many generations, for no one would call the prizes extravagant. Membership cost 2s. a year, and it is recorded with pride in the minutes that in the year 1802 the entire funds of the society were spent in buying flannel waistcoats for the Paisley Volunteers. In 1794 there were 42 members, in 1883 about 100. Their motto is "There is a wondrous pleasure in the cultivation of flowers".

This society has certainly lived up to it. Not satisfied with one society, Paisley at one period could boast of no less than five which were active at the same time.

Our most important society, the Royal Caledonian Horticultural Society, has passed through many vicissitudes. It was founded on December 5, 1809, when seventeen men assembled in the Physicians' Hall "to constitute themselves into a Society for encouraging and improving the cultivation of the best fruit, of the most choice flowers and most useful culinary vegetables".[48] The first exhibit was that of James Macdonald, head gardener at Dalkeith, who on December 19 of the same year exhibited blanched Seakale and read a short paper on its cultivation.

The society owes a great debt to its past secretary, Mr Donald Mackenzie, for his researches into its very interesting history. He draws attention to its early task of holding competitions for home-made wines, which were very popular during the Napoleonic wars. In 1811 24 different kinds of wine were judged, which rose to 34 in 1812. Their public spirit was shown by their offer in 1814 of a prize of five guineas to any inhabitant of Edinburgh who should make for sale the greatest quantity of Currant wine, so as to remove the danger of a glut on the market caused by an exceedingly abundant crop of White Currants. This was won by a Mr George Montgomery who paid duty on no less than $866\frac{1}{2}$ gallons.

In its early days the society often offered special prizes or premiums for special efforts or new ideas. For instance, an award was made in 1814 for a woollen net which was said to be excellent for preserving fruit blossom from late spring frosts.

Unfortunately the society was too ambitious and for many years spent more than its income. One excessive item for a small society was the formation of a trial garden on ground which has since been incorporated in the Royal Botanic Garden at Inverleith. This garden was started about 1823, and within a few years the financial troubles of the society began. Evening Promenades were held weekly to try and raise funds but without any success, and their prodigal spending was pilloried in the *Scotsman*. Their position was not improved by the formation in the late twenties of two other horticultural societies. Nevertheless the council went on steadily. In 1842 a Horticultural Hall was built, which now forms the Herbarium at Inverleith, while about 1853 two Camellia houses were built. Such prodigal spending could only have one end: in 1856 the garden was offered to the Government, but negotiations were protracted and acrimonious, and it was not until 1865 that the garden was finally handed over.[48]

Meanwhile the society had always taken a great interest in flower and fruit shows, which were frequently held. They may not have been a financial success, but undoubtedly they helped the spread of gardening in every direction. This was before the days of the great power of the Royal Horticultural Society, and gardeners were in the habit of staging as fine exhibits in Edinburgh as are to be seen to-day in London. International Shows were held in 1865, 1869, 1875, 1882 and 1891.

Although the actual originator may have been an

eccentric individual, Dr. Andrew Duncan, the main-spring of its early activities was Patrick Neill. A printer by trade, he was a most enthusiastic gardener, with a most remarkable knowledge of Scottish gardens and horticulture.

Later in the nineteenth century many other societies were formed, such as that in Dundee in 1824 and others in small villages like New Pitsligo in Aberdeenshire in 1840.

By the middle of the century flower-shows were extremely popular. Some were devoted to particular favourites, such as Hollyhocks, Picotees and Dahlias, while the Pansy was sufficiently the rage to have its own society, in addition to having several classes devoted to it at every show in season, however small the society may have been. Greenhouse plants were much in evidence, particularly Camellias, Cape Heaths and Epacris. Other popular show plants were Auriculas, Cinerarias and Indian Azaleas which at that time were imported into Scotland in large quantities by Van Houtte.

An average schedule for a summer show was:

2 shrubby greenhouse plants	4 Phloxes
2 Fuchsias, one dark, one light	3 stage Pelargoniums
2 Achimenes	3 fancy Pelargoniums
Exotic Heaths	24 cut Roses
3 pairs of Pinks	6 Calceolarias [69]

You will note the preponderance of greenhouse plants; and yet this show was held in Dunfermline, not in Edinburgh or Glasgow. The Dunfermline Horticultural Society was very much alive and saw

197

that its shows were well reported in the press. One journalist ended up a fulsome account with: "Others sent in plants to grace the hall, including a very elegant and unique Chinese cage, containing a pretty Canary bird". This same society was in the habit of granting First Class Certificates for new plants, which shows how localized was life in general, even as late as 1850. There was no idea in their minds of running counter to any of the larger societies, which at that time were by no means in a flourishing condition, but gardeners rarely travelled far afield and the carriage of plants in good condition over long distances was almost an impossibility. New plants were often shown at local shows almost as early as they were seen in London. For instance, a Mr Falconer received a special prize for *Primula sikkimensis* in 1852, only two years after its introduction.

These horticultural societies and flower-shows did yeoman service in popularizing gardening in general. Those in small towns and country districts are as active to-day; it is only a pity that some of the societies in larger towns are losing their influence, for societies and their flower-shows are always stimulating to local effort.

CHAPTER X

The Gardener

SCOTLAND was famed for its gardeners before the outside world knew that there was a garden in Scotland. Why this should have been has long been a puzzle. It was a problem that worried the worthy Switzer, was commented upon by Tobias Smollett, and caused trouble towards the end of the eighteenth century when English gardeners complained that Scotsmen were usurping their places.

The answer usually given is that Scottish parochial education was better than that in England: a meaningless explanation. It has been mentioned before how unimaginative were Scottish school-teachers and ministers about anything to do with the soil. A thorough grounding in elementary education, even if it had been superior in Scotland, might have made worthy citizens, but it would not have made expert gardeners in a country where horticulture and its kindred sciences were anything but a universal pursuit.

From such references as exist to gardeners before the Restoration it is clear that Scotsmen at home had little opportunity of acquiring expert knowledge. In England gardeners had a long native and Continental tradition behind them; in Scotland there was none. Before the Reformation the monks supplied the brains and the experience, while such names of skilled men as have come down to us either belonged to the Church or were Frenchmen; most natives who are mentioned in the Exchequer Rolls or in old papers were little better than garden labourers who had to produce small crops of fruit and vegetables for appetites that were easily satisfied. After the Reformation we hear little of the men who actually worked the garden, until we come to the Restoration.

A minor problem has been mentioned before. Where did John Reid, author of *The Scots Gard'ner*, gain his experience? His name must be coupled with that of James Sutherland, the first Intendent of the Botanic Garden in Edinburgh, as the two foremost gardeners of their time in Scotland. Reid's knowledge was beyond what could have been gained in any of our own big gardens, and yet from internal evidence in his book one would say that his knowledge was honourably come by; that is, from his own experience, for his book does not read like a symposium. One can only suspect from the contents and language that he gained some of his experience in England.

Large gardens were made so rapidly and with so sure a hand after the Restoration that there cannot have been sufficient talent at home to supply the demand for trained head gardeners. Is it unreasonable to suppose that many positions were filled by repatriated Scots who had filled similar positions in England, and even abroad? It is known that English garden designers helped to lay out a number of

Scottish gardens: in some cases a man was sent north to superintend the work, and they may have remained as head gardeners. It is odd, however, that we rarely hear of English gardeners in Scotland, although very often of Scottish gardeners in England. It might appear at first glance that this was a matter of little importance; but it is partly due to the influence of our gardener immigrants that horticulture has reached such a high standard in our country.

Gardeners who have left the country to work elsewhere have always been nationally minded. We are a clannish people, and wherever they may have found themselves they have always been willing and eager to help horticulture in Scotland with their advice, experience and, wherever possible, with practical gifts of seeds and plants. This practice has been going on for over two hundred years, and it still continues.

That a great many Scotsmen held high positions in gardens in England during the eighteenth century is abundantly proved. Switzer wrote in 1718: "There are several Northern Lads, which whether they have serv'd time in their Art, or not, very few of us know anything of; yet by the help of a little Learning, and a great deal of Impudence they invade these Southern Provinces; and the natural benignity of this warmer climate has such a wonderful influence on them, that one of them knows (or at least pretends to know) more in one twelve-month, than a laborious, honest *South* Country man does in seven years". That is a bitter complaint of which the cause could not have arisen in a year or two. Switzer, who was a fair-minded man, would not have written with such venom if they had been mere labourers, or even journeymen gardeners; they must have held high positions.

Then as a second example of the frequency with which this subject is mentioned, there is a quotation from the *Autobiography of Dr. Alexander Carlyle*, himself a Scotsman: "It was at Bulstrode that we discovered the truth of what I had often heard, that most of the head-gardeners of English noblemen were Scotch. This man was not only gardener but land-steward, and had the charge of the whole park and of the estate around it."[12] He also mentioned that the head gardener at Blenheim was a Scotsman.

Ill feeling, which must have simmered for years, came to a head when Scotsmen began, about 1760, to make a success of nursery gardening near London. Then the English in retaliation rushed into print and attacked Scottish gardeners tooth and nail. They also tried to resuscitate an old Chartered Company of Gardeners under a Charter of James I. A resolution was passed at an early meeting that no apprentice from the north should be employed. In time the agitation passed. Since then many Scots have moved south as gardeners, and, let us hope, have worked amicably with their English brethren.

This steady emigration must have been due to several causes. It is true both in agriculture and horticulture that a man will naturally tend to drift to a softer and more equable climate, where conditions are easier and plants of all kinds respond more rapidly to care and attention. It is also true that an employer is willing, indeed often prefers, to obtain his labour from a less happy climate than his own.

He considers that a man who has been trained in an unkindly climate will by nature work harder than one who has lived all his life under comparatively easier conditions. Thus there tends to be a constant movement southwards.

In our history there were at least three occasions between 1603 and 1707 when emigration to England was possible from historical causes. The first was the accession of James VI to the Throne of England, the second the Restoration, the third the Union of the two countries. During this period, when it was becoming a commoner occurrence to find large landowners owning estates in both countries, there was a certain movement from one estate to another.

The great influx, however, of Scottish gardeners to England undoubtedly began during the period of Philip Miller. This excellent gardener, who was himself a Scotsman, became Curator of the Physic Garden at Chelsea given by Sir Hans Sloane in 1722 to the Apothecaries Company. Miller was quite definite in his preference for his own countrymen. They were brought south to act as apprentices, and when trained obtained good positions elsewhere through Miller's influence. When they reached the post of head gardener on some big English estate, they in their turn sent north for more apprentices; and so it went on. William Aiton the elder, who made the original Royal Botanic Garden at Kew, was one of Miller's apprentices.

Finally, there was more chance of advancement in the south. The Scottish working man of the eighteenth and early nineteenth centuries was more ambitious than the similar class in England. He was anxious to better himself and grasped every opportunity that came his way. Under the Scottish system the life of an apprentice was as a rule harder and longer in the north than in the south. On the other hand, there seems to have been great willingness on the part of some head gardeners to impart their knowledge and experience to their juniors; William McNab, the principal Gardener at the Royal Botanic Garden at Edinburgh from 1810 to 1848 was a case in point, and so was James McDonald, head gardener at Dalkeith. In many large gardens classes for apprentices played a regular part in their training. A great many failed to take advantage of this excellent chance either from stupidity or lack of ambition, but the number who tried their hardest to better themselves was very large, far too large for possible vacancies in Scotland. Just as in the years 1919 to 1929 many first-class Scottish gardeners found immediate employment in the United States, so from about 1700 to 1850 there must have been a constant flow of trained men from Scotland to England.

It is really surprising that the trade of gardener was so popular in Scotland. On the whole, conditions of work and wages were bad, until towards the end of the last century. In a former chapter a list is given of wages paid at Dalkeith during the year 1813. Dalkeith at that time was probably the largest garden in Scotland, yet the head gardener received a wage of only £88. William McNab, one of the greatest gardeners that Scotland has produced, was paid £50 per annum when he was appointed to Edinburgh

in 1810: it was many years before this was increased
to £3 a week. Foremen, skilled men in their departments, were paid 12s. a week; journeymen, from 6s.
to 10s.; apprentices, 6d. a day. In addition, almost
all apprentices and many journeymen had to pay
premiums to the head gardener ranging from £5 to
£10 which were usually deducted in instalments from
their wages.

By 1860 wages had increased. Journeymen were
paid 15s. a week and apprentices 9s., but conditions
of labour were just as bad. No half holidays were
granted, unless under exceptional circumstances,
while hours of work were quite unregulated. Un-
married men lived in bothies, communal establishments where they had to keep themselves, a practice
still common in Scotland; but the bothies up to 1860
were just hovels, usually built under the north wall
of the garden. Complaints were frequent: here is one
from a foreman gardener in 1862: "I am aware of late
years much has been done to improve these; but there
still remains much to be done. Many of our bothies
are low, damp, ill-ventilated hovels, consisting of a
single room, into which the sun's cheering rays
seldom or never penetrate. Into such places four, or
perhaps more, young men are thrust, where they
have to sleep, eat, and prepare all the necessaries of
life. If they wish to be alone they must go to the
woods or the fields."[69]

Yet the gardening trade in Scotland has been
really popular. It has attracted to it in the last two
hundred years an excellent type of man, not afraid to
work with his own hands however high his position,

205

a good organizer, self-reliant and thoroughly trust-worthy. If some may have been a trifle lacking in imagination and have been dour, yet they were often saved by a pawky humour; as, for instance, the old gardener in Dean Ramsay's famous story who, when told that it was time that he retired, answered, "Na, Na; I'm no gangin'. If ye dinna ken whan ye've a gude servant, I ken when I've a gude place."

William McNab can be taken as a perfect example of the type. Born in 1780 in the parish of Dailly in Ayrshire, he was apprenticed at the age of 16 in the garden of a Mr Kennedy at Dalquharran in Carrick. Three years later he moved to Tyninghame, and at 21 went to Kew where William Aiton appointed him a foreman of the Royal Gardens at the early age of 23.

Meanwhile the Royal Botanic Garden at Edin-burgh had been passing through a lean time. McNab was offered the post of head gardener in 1810 at the suggestion of Sir Joseph Banks and Mr Aiton. It says much for his enthusiasm that he accepted it for the pittance of £50 a year, with the possibility of another £10 in perquisites.

From the start he was a great success. He was responsible for the successful removal during 1821 and 1822 of the gardens from their old site in Leith Walk to the present situation at Inverleith. His general lay-out both in plant and houses was admir-able, while the actual transplantation could not have been bettered. Lord Cockburn wrote: "No garden could be made to walk a mile with less injury to its health. Scarcely a single plant or tree was lost, and after recovering from their first sickness, they looked fresher and prouder than ever."

Once he was settled at Inverleith his influence on Scottish gardening was supreme. In the Botanic Garden he increased the collection of exotics and made it of great value to all Scottish horticulture. He was particularly successful with greenhouse plants, and the collection of Cape Heaths and those stove genera which were known as New Holland Plants was unrivalled.

He wrote a rare pamphlet on the subject, called *The Cultivation of Cape Heaths*. It was stated in the *Hortus Woburnensis* that this "contains the most valuable instruction that has ever yet appeared in print on the subject, and ought to be in the hands of every cultivator or admirer of Ericaceae; it is rendered doubly valuable by its coming from the pen of one who is generally known to be one of the best practical botanists and most successful cultivators in Britain, and whose heaths are actually grown to the size of small trees, and many of them covered, from the edge of the pots to the extremity of the plants, with beautiful blossoms".

McNab himself wrote that "There are in the Botanic Garden at Edinburgh, heaths grown 8 feet high, in tubs 3 feet over, and the plants are bushy in proportion to their height and in great vigour; and these, when in flower, are covered with blossoms from the edge of the tubs to the top of the plants". Contemporaries bear out that this was no exaggeration.

He was equally successful with outdoor plants, particularly with the transplanting of evergreens.

McNab was of the best type of Scottish head gardener, austere and yet kindly, hard-working, conscientious, learning his work and his plants by practical observation and experience, willing to give of his great knowledge to others, and, above all, completely trustworthy. It is a pity that his name is almost forgotten.

Naturally there were all kinds and conditions of gardeners, from the type of McNab to the pompous snob who could write that "The harsh incorrect style of uneducated persons must vibrate very disagreeably in the ears of accomplished and refined society".[69] In the middle of the century there was a long and acrimonious discussion in the Scottish gardening press on the various qualities with which a head gardener should be endowed. One anonymous writer after praising at length the perfect type, with McNab as the example, went on to classify head gardeners whom he considered unfortunate or unsatisfactory: "Let us first consider the man of habits and routine, the unreasoning, hand-to-mouth gardener. This is very often a very worthy sort of man. His garden is generally in tolerable if not first-rate order. He is, however, altogether an empiric. He follows rules with slavish exactness, but does not know the reasons for them. His models are what he saw in his apprenticeship, or when he was foreman. He is kept much at home, and so does not see what his neighbours are doing. Above all, he is overworked; he has a garden to keep with insufficient means. Mastered by circumstances he is always in what an old friend used to call 'a guddle'."[69]

The author disliked the specialists of the day: "They are not happy unless they are engaged in the highest departments of the art. They feel themselves only second-chop gardeners, as the Chinese would phrase it, if they had not command of Pine-stoves, Vineries, Peach-houses and all the other appliances of forcing. If one of these is wanting, they are ideally not complete. Suppose a man of this kind is appointed to an old place: he roots out and demolishes a time-consecrated garden, and converts it into a ribband parterre. He betakes himself to landscape gardening when his employer wants his table to be filled with fruit and vegetables. He runs off to Dahlia shows while potatoes are deficient in the kitchen."

But mostly is he against the head gardener who kept his underlings working at high pressure in watertight compartments. "Suppose that a famous garden is superintended by a very distinguished master gardener. It is an object of ambition with young men to get there. To have been at this garden stamps a youthful gardener with consequence; to be a favourite with the great man there is a sure pass-port to success in life. After a preliminary trial to see what is in him, he is put in charge of some limited department, for which he is made responsible. He is told, perhaps, here are three vineries; if you need help, you will get it on application; but if a single leaf is sun-struck or blistered, you will have to seek another situation. To be dismissed from this garden is far worse than never to have been there at all. To avoid that a young man will work from five in the morning to nine at night. He will be so absorbed in

P

his vineries that he will hardly have a glimpse of aught else in the garden, and so, except in the matter of Grape growing, he gets no experience; and what is worse, comes to believe that the system is an excellent one, and adopts it as his own when he is no longer a fag, but a master. And the same method is carried through all the departments in the garden."

Unfortunately that last method was common in great Victorian gardens, particularly in indoor departments where cultivation was brought to such a high pitch of excellence. Nevertheless it had its good points; it taught a young gardener responsibility at an early age; it also taught him the technique of one department with great thoroughness. Whether the head gardener was tyrannical or was always in "a guddle", the general result of the teaching of our head gardener has, on the whole, been excellent. If it had not been for our professional class of gardeners, Scottish horticulture would not be in the proud position it holds to-day.

APPENDIX A

Weights and Measures

In most cases Scottish measures differed from those in England; not only so, but they varied in different towns and districts. This is not a matter of great importance in the history of gardening, but it shows how difficult it is to understand old computations of crops, etc.

1 Scottish Acre = 160 Falls = 6150·5 Square Yards.
1 English Acre = 4840 Square Yards.
1 Scots Pint, 2⅓ lbs. (about) for vegetables.
1 Boll (flour) = 140 lbs.
1 Boll (grain or meal) = 448 lbs.
1 Peck (Potatoes) = 12 Scots Pints.
1 Peck Peas, Onions, etc.) in Edinburgh = 28 lbs.
1 Peck   ,,   ,,   ,,   in Cupar = 20 lbs.
1 Peck   ,,   ,,   ,,   in Glasgow = 42 lbs.
1 Peck   ,,   ,,   ,,   in Renfrewshire = 35 lbs.
1 Peck (fruit measure), 24 Scots Pints = 56 lbs.
1 Sleek was usually 18 Scots Pints, about 42 lbs., but in Dundee
1 Sleek of Apples weighed 40 lbs.
1 Sleek of Pears   ,,   50 lbs.
1 Sleek of Plums   ,,   56 lbs.

Seedlings were almost always sold at 120 for the hundred, while in vegetables sold by number a long hundred varied from 120 to as much as 178 in the Edinburgh market.

Thus it will be seen in what a hopeless muddle were Scottish measures for garden and orchard produce.

211

APPENDIX B

A Collection of Seed sent by Mr Wright from Quebec to the Society for Importation of Foreign Seeds in 1768 (see p. 115)

1. Great White Spruce—for beer and plank. 80 feet.
   Picea canadensis (Mill.) B.S.P.

2. Great Black Spruce—true sort for spruce beer. 50 feet.
   Picea mariana (Mill.) B.S.P.

3. Red Spruce—for beer and plank. 100 feet
   Picea rubra (Du Roi) Dietr.

4. White Pine—good deal. 60 feet.
   Pinus strobus. L.

5. Balsam Fir—for a balsam got by Indians. 60 feet.
   Abies balsamea (L.) Miller.

6. Great Black Larix—beams, etc. for building. 80 feet.
   Larix laricina (Du Roi) Koch.

7. Great Red Larix
   Possibly Red Cedar, *Juniperus*

8. Great White Larix
   Virginiana (L.) and White Cedar, *Thuja occidentalis* (L.).

9. White Ash—for carts, ploughs, calashes, etc. 100 feet.
   Fraxinus americana L.

10. Gray Ash—
> Name not found. The Black Ash *F. nigra* Marsh grows abundantly in the country surrounding Quebec. The wood is softer and weaker than that of the white ash, but is used.

11. Mapple of Canada.
> Name not found. It seems reasonable to suppose, however, that it was applied to the Sugar Maple, *Acer saccharum* Marsh, also known as Rock and Hard Maple, which is the species of greatest importance as a timber tree and for the high sugar content of its sap.

12. Red Mapple—fine plank and sugar juice. 100 feet.
> *Acer rubrum* Linn.

13. Red ditto called Red Platanus. 100 feet.
> Doubtless the same as No. 12.

14. Yellow ditto, rare. 100 feet.
> Possibly the same as No. 12.

15. White ditto called Platanus. 100 feet.
> *Acer saccharinum* Linn.

16. Another called White Mapple. 100 feet.
> Doubtless the same as No. 15.

17. A tree called Berry-bearing Poplar. 135 feet.
> Name not found. *Populus balsamifera* L. has buds that "are large and sealed with a fragrant, sticky gum". These might be likened to "berries". However, it is not common for it to reach 135 feet; such a height would be the exception rather than the rule.

18. Red Poplar.
    Name not found. Cannot suggest a connection.

19. Great White Elm—bark used by Indians for ropes. 120 feet.
    Ulmus americana Linn.

20. Great Red Elm—ditto. 120 feet.
    Ulmus fulva Michx.

21. Red Mespilus—eat as apples by natives. 40 feet.
    The name Mespilus I have not come across. It would
    seem likely at least that *Crataegus coccineus* Linn.
    is referred to. This is called by the French Cana-
    dians "Pommetier Rouge".

22. Great White Mespilus. 40 feet.
    Possibly *Crataegus tomentosa* Linn. called in French
    "pommetiere jaune". The qualifying adjective
    "white" may have reference to the flowers or to the
    whiteness of the branches due to tomentum.

23. Scarlet Hornbeam—for making ploughs and barrows. 30
    feet.
    Possibly *Ostrya virginiana* (Mill.) K. Koch.

24. Black Hop Hornbeam—ditto.
    Possibly synonymous with the preceding.

25. Red Birch—plank, vinegar made from juice. 100 feet.
    Most likely *Betula lutea* Michx.

26. Great Black Birch—best sort for planks. 100 feet.
    Possibly *B. lenta* Linn., but as likely *B. lutea*. *B. lenta*
    only occasionally reaches a height of 75 feet.

27. White Birch—bark for making canoes. 100 feet.
    Betula alba L. var. *papyrifera* (Marsh) Spach.

214

28. Great Line—for making wigwams. 120 feet.
    Tilia americana Linn.

29. Broad-leaved Beech.
    Possibly *Fagus grandifolia* Ehrh.

30. Oak with rough empalement—the best sort of oak and rare. 120 feet.
    Most likely *Quercus alba* Linn.

31. Great Hagberry.
    Celtis occidentalis Linn.

32. Hickory Walnuts—fine plank, very much used. 80 feet.
    Carya cordiformis (Wang.) Koch. or *Carya ovata* (Mill.) Koch. More likely the former.

33. Black ditto—very fine plank.
    It seems impossible that the real Black Walnut, *Juglans nigra* Linn., is the tree referred to. Its natural distribution is restricted to a very small area in southern Ontario, the most easterly point being some three hundred miles west of Quebec city. On the other hand the Butternut, *Juglans cinerea* Linn., extends to within a short distance of Quebec. Even to-day it is commonly spoken of as the Black Walnut. I am therefore of the opinion that *J. cinerea* is the tree, not *J. nigra*.

[I have to thank Mr Arthur Kellett of the Government Experimental Farm at Ottawa for supplying the probable modern equivalents and the notes given above.—E. H. M. C.]

APPENDIX C

*A Typical Invoice for the Yearly Supply of Seeds of about
1820 to Colonel Boyle, Irvine*

6 lbs Early france pease	2/6	
6 lbs White Roncival do	2/–	
4 lbs Green Imperial do	1/4	
4 lbs Spanish Morotto do	1/4	
6 lbs Early Charlton do	1/6	
4 lbs Tall Marrowfat do	1/4	
4 lbs Large Crooked Sugar do	4/–	
3 lbs Green Friessian do	1/–	
2 lbs New Blue Prolific do	10d	
2 lbs New Nonpareil do	10d	
6 lbs Large Windsor Beans	2/–	
½ lb Early White Kidney do	8d	
½ lb Speckled Kidney do	8d	
4 lbs Long Pod Beans	1/2	
4 ozs Scarlet Runner	4d	
1 lb Deptford Onion	4/6	
1 lb Strasburgh Onion	3/6	
6 ozs James Keeping do	2/6	
½ lb Early Dutch Horn Carrot	2/–	
½ lb Large Orange do	1/–	
½ lb Long Red Carrot	1/–	
2 ozs Altringham do	8d	
½ lb yellow Dutch Turnip	1/3	
2 ozs yellow Stone do	5d	
½ lb Early Dutch do	1/6	
2 ozs Early White Stone do	4d	
1 oz New Early do	3d	
4 ozs Early York Cabbage	2/6	
1 oz Large Scots do	3d	
2 ozs Early Dwf do	1/6	
2 ozs Sugarloaf do	1/–	
1 oz Red Dutch do	8d	
1 oz New Early do	8d	
½ oz Early Cape Broccoli	1/–	
½ oz Dwf Purple do	8d	
½ oz Late Sulphur do	8d	
½ oz Early Malta do	9d	
½ oz Hardy Green do	8d	

½ oz Late White Broccoli		8d
2 ozs German Green		6d
1 oz Dwf Green		3d
1 oz Brussels Sprouts		8d
1 oz Green Curled Savoy		3d
1 oz Yellow do		4d
4 Dr Red Solid Cellery		4d
4 Dr White Solid Cellery		4d
2 ozs Red Beet		6d
1 oz White do		3d
½ oz Large Green Cos Lettuce		8d
1 oz Drumhead do	1/6	
1 oz Early Cauliflower	2/3	
1 oz Parsnip		3d
½ lb White Mustard		8d
2 ozs Early Frame Radish		4d
1 oz Red Turnip do		3d
2 ozs Scarlet Salmon do		4d
1 oz White Turnip do		3d
3 ozs Large Scots Leek	2/–	
3 ozs Flag do	1/6	
½ oz Summer Savory		8d
½ oz Thyme		8d
1 lb Round Spinage	1/–	

Flowers

2 ozs Indian Cress	1/–	
6 ozs Mixed Sweet Pease	10d	
2 ozs Mignonette	2/–	
1 oz Yellow Lupins		6d
1 oz Dutch Blue Lupins		6d
2 ozs Small Blue Lupins		8d
1 oz Straw Coloured Lupins		6d
59 Sorts Hardy Annuals	14/9	
15 Sorts Tender Annuals	7/6	
15 Sorts Perennials	3/9	
1 Matt and Package	1/–	

APPENDIX D

List of Annuals suggested by an Amateur in 1855 (see p. 128)

Ageratum coelestinum
„ *odoratum*
Alyssum calycinum
Anagallis
Aster sinensis
Brachycome iberidifolia
Clarkia elegans
„ *pulchella*
Clintonia pulchella
Collinsia bicolor
„ *grandiflora*
Convolvulus tricolor
Dianthus sinensis
Erysimum Perowskianum
Eschscholtzia californica
„ *crocea*
Everlastings
Gilia achillaeafolia
„ *tricolor*
Iberis coronaria
„ *umbellata*
Kaulfussia amelloides
Larkspur
Leptosiphon densiflorus
„ *androsaceus*

Lobelia erimoides
„ *ramosa*
Lupinus nanus
„ *Hartwegii*
„ *mutabilis*
Marigold, African
„ double
„ French
Mignonette
Nemophila insignis
„ *maculata*
Petunia nyctaginiflora
„ *violacea*
Phlox Drummondii
Platystemon californicum
Portulacca grandiflora
Salpiglossis
Sanvitalia procumbens
Saponaria calabrica
Scabiosa atropurpurea
Schizanthus
Senecio elegans
Stock, Ten Week
„ Virginian
Viscaria occulata

217

GLOSSARY

Beetchard—Swiss Beet

Beetrave—Beetroot

Bere—Barley

Birk—Birch

Blazie—Baron's deputy

Boure—bower

Byer or *byre*—cowhouse

Castin dikis—make walls

Clairie—*Salvia Sclarea*

Coste—coast

Dubis—small pools

Geintrie—the Gean, *Prunus Avium*

Grasman—tenant of cottage without land attached

Hollins—Hollies

Hou—hoe

Imp—a scion for a graft

Kail—generic name for Colewort

Lib. See **Pound**

Merk—a silver coin worth about 1s. 1⅓d. sterling

Myre—bog

Perfit—perfect

Plyed—trained

Pompion—Pumpkin

Pound (*Scots*)—about 1s. 6d. sterling

Purpie—Purple Kail

Quheit—Wheat

Rockambole—*Allium Scorodoprasum*

Rountrie—Mountain Ash

Run-rigging—ten-foot ridges in fields worked by different tenants

Sairing—satisfying

Saphorn—Saffron

Sauch—Willow

Schoon—shoes

Shilling (*Scots*)—about 1d. sterling

Skirret—*Sium Sisarum*

Sueit—sweet

Tacksman—a leaseholder

Tarrass—terrace

Wopen—bundled

Yearde—garden

BIBLIOGRAPHY

1. Anon., *Ways and Means of Enclosing.* 1729.
2. *Baillie, Lady Grizel, The Household Book of.* Scottish History Society, 1692–1733. 1911.
3. Bannatyne Club, Publications of. Various volumes.
4. Barrett, Michael, *The Scottish Monasteries of Old.* 1913.
5. Batten, E. Chisholm, *History of Beauly Priory.* 1877.
6. Brown, Prof. Hume, *Early Travellers in Scotland.* 1891.
7. Brown, Prof. Hume, *Scotland before 1700, from Contemporary Documents.* 1893.
8. Brown, Prof. Hume, *Scotland in the Time of Queen Mary.* 1904.
9. Brown, Robert, *The History of Paisley.* 1884.
10. *Caledonian Horticultural Society, Memoirs of.* 4 vols. 1814–1829.
11. Campbell, James, *Balmerino Abbey.* 1867.
12. *Carlyle, Dr. Alexander, The Autobiography of,* 1722–1770. 1860
13. Cecil, The Hon. Mrs Evelyn, *A History of Gardening in England.* 3rd ed. 1910.
14. Chalmers, George, *Caledonia Depicta.* 4 vols. 1807.
15. Cobbett, William, *Rural Rides.*
16. Cochran-Patrick, R. W., *Mediaeval Scotland.* 1892.
17. Cockburn, John—*Letters of John Cockburn to his Gardener.* Edited by James Colville. Scottish History Society. 1904.
18. Coltness Collections. Maitland Club. 1842.
19. *Country Life.* Various volumes.
20. Dalkeith, Various MS. Accounts of.
21. Defoe, Daniel, *A Tour thro' the whole Island of Great Britain.* 1724.
22. Dicksons & Co., Various MS. Account Books and Catalogues.
23. Douglas, Sir Robert, *Peerage of Scotland.* 1764.
24. Dunbar, James, *Social Life in Former Days.* 2 vols. 1865.
25. Dunkeld—*Rentale Dunkeldense, 1505–1517.* Scottish History Society. 1915.
26. Edinburgh—*Notes from the Royal Botanic Garden.* Various numbers.
27. *Edinburgh Philosophical Journal.* Various volumes.

28. Edinburgh—*The Royal Botanic Garden, A Brief Descriptive and Illustrated Account.* 1934.

29. Foulis—*Account Book of Sir John Foulis of Ravelston,* 1671–1707. Scottish History Society.

30. *Gardeners' Magazine, The.* Various volumes.

31. Gilpin, William, *Observations on the Picturesque.* 2 vols. 1776.

32. Glasgow—*Companion to the Glasgow Botanic Garden.* N.D.

33. Gordon, Sir Robert, *Notes for Blau's Atlas.* 1654.

34. Graham, Henry Grey, *The Social Life in Scotland in the Eighteenth Century.* 6th ed. 1928.

35. Haldane, Elizabeth S., *Scots Gardens in Old Times.* 1934.

36. Home, Henry, Lord Kames, *Elements of Criticism,* 9th ed. 1817.

37. Home, Henry, Lord Kames, *The Gentleman Farmer.* 1776.

38. Hunter, Thomas, *Woods, Forests and Estates of Perthshire.* 1883.

39. Justice, James, *The Scots Gardener's Director.* 1754.

40. Lawson & Son, Peter, Various Catalogues.

41. Lindsay, Lord, *The Lives of the Lindsays.* 3 vols. 1849.

42. Logan, James, *The Scottish Gael.* 2 vols. 1831.

43. Lothian, James, *Alpines or Rock Plants.* 1845.

44. Loudon, J. C., *Arboretum et Fruticetum Brittanicum.* 8 vols. 1838.

45. Loudon, J. C., *Encyclopedia of Gardening.* New edition. 1878.

46. Lowther, C., *Our Journall into Scotland in 1629.* Printed 1894.

47. MacGibbon, D. and Ross, T., *The Castellated and Domestic Architecture of Scotland.* 5 vols. 1887.

48. Mackenzie, Donald, *The History of the Royal Caledonian Horticultural Society.* Ex. Trans. 1935.

49. Macky, John, *A Journey through Scotland.* 2nd ed. 1732.

50. Maitland, Sir Richard, *History of the House of Seyton.* 1829.

51. Maxwell, Sir Herbert, *Scottish Gardens.* 1908.

52. Morer, Thomas, *A Short Account of Scotland,* 1689.

53. Neill, Patrick, *Journal of a Horticultural Tour through some Parts of Flanders, Holland and the North of France.* 1823.

54. Neill, Patrick, *On Scottish Gardens and Orchards.* 1812.

55. Neill, Patrick, *The Fruit, Flower and Kitchen Garden.* 5th ed. 1854.

56. Nicol, Walter, *The Villa-Garden Directory.* 1823.

57. Omond, George, *Arniston Memoirs.* 3 vols. 1887.

58. Pennant, Thomas, *A Tour in Scotland and a Voyage to the Hebrides.* 1774.

59. *Proceedings of the Society of Antiquaries of Scotland.* Various volumes.
60. Ramage, Craufurd Tait, *Drumlanrig Castle and the Douglases.* 1876.
61. Reid, John, *The Scots Gard'ner.* 1683.
62. Rogers, C., *Rental Book of Cupar Angus Abbey.* 2 vols. 1879.
63. Scotland—Accounts of the Lord High Treasurer.
64. *Scotland, Exchequer Rolls of.* Various volumes from 1400.
65. Scotland—*Proceedings of the Society of Antiquaries.* Various volumes.
66. *Scotland, The New Statistical Account of.* 1845.
67. *Scots Magazine, The.* Various volumes.
68. Scott, Sir Walter, "Landscape Gardening", *Quarterly Review*, vol. xxxvii.
69. *Scottish Gardener, The.* 15 vols. 1852–1867.
70. *Scottish Historical Review, The.* 1903–1907.
71. Sherry, Christopher, *The Glasgow Botanic Garden, its Conservatories, Greenhouses, etc.*
72. *Spalding Club Miscellanies.* Various volumes.
73. Stuart, John, *Records of the Abbey of Kinloss.*
74. Thomson, Thomas, *The Scottish Seed Trade of 1784.* 1934.
75. Urie—*Court Book of the Barony of Urie.* Scottish History Society.

INDEX OF PLACES

223

INDEX

INDEX

THE END

Printed in Great Britain by R. & R. CLARK, LIMITED, *Edinburgh.*